An unofficial practical guide to Boy
Scouting for parents and new leaders

Beginning Boy Scouts

Heather R. Reed
Jeremy C. Reed

Beginning Boy Scouts
By Jeremy C. Reed and Heather R. Reed

Copyright © 2011 Jeremy C. Reed

Publisher: Reed Media Services
http://www.reedmedia.net/
September 2011

ISBN 978-1-937516-01-7

Cover design by Getty Creations

Contents

Preface

This book is an introduction to the youth program of the Boy Scouts of America. It is an unofficial guide to Boy Scouting to help parents, new leaders, and even scouting youth to better understand scouting goals and participate in Boy Scouting. It quickly answers numerous common questions and provides instruction and advice for concerned and desperate parents and leaders — to help know "what is first?" and how to get started, preparing for outdoor activities and summer camp, uniforms, leadership and the *Patrol Method*, earning awards and badges, Eagle planning, Eagle paperwork, and how to participate. It introduces the terminology and defines the common scouting lingo.

The purpose of this book is not to replace official Boy Scouts of America materials or training — we encourage leaders to attend and complete official training. In addition to the sage advice for new and experienced parents and scoutmasters, this book includes references to point parents and leaders to other instruction.

Note that many terms and designs related to Boy Scouting are trademarked or proprietary to the Boy Scouts of America. This book is not an official book from the BSA.

For updated information and website links, please visit `http://www.reedmedia.net/books/beginning-boy-scouts/`.

About the Authors

The authors, Jeremy C. Reed and Heather R. Reed, are parents of seven sons and one daughter. They live near Fort Worth, Texas, where he is an 11-year-old Scout Leader and she serves as a Cub Scout Committee Chair. Their family enjoys camping, hiking, and educational and adventurous road trips. Jeremy is an open source software advocate and Heather is a stay-at-home mom.

Acknowledgments

Thank you to our technical reviewers and contributors: Catie Watson, volunteer, Pacifica District, Orange County Council; John Hearing, volunteer Scouter, Chief Seattle Council; Shawn Elder, District Commissioner, Superstition District, Grand Canyon Council; Damon Edmondson, Assistant Council Commissioner, Atlanta Area Council; and Corinna Jones, Unit Commissioner, Sunset District, Great Lakes Council. We are also grateful to several others who provided helpful feedback.

Upcoming Books

Reed Media Services, a publisher of over ten books, is working on *Beginning Cub Scouts*, a book focused on helping parents and new leaders learn about the Cub Scouting program. The book covers finding and joining a pack, what happens at pack and den meetings, the uniform and supplies, fundamental steps in earning badges and awards, day camps, and how to volunteer. For more information, visit `http://www.reedmedia.` `net/books/beginning-cub-scouts/`.

The authors of this book are also writing about *planning successful family road trips*. Traveling with a family provides great opportunities for family bonding, education, and expanding perspective. This book will share suggestions, guidelines, and experiences with planning and achieving fun short- and long-term family road trips — with a focus on car touring with children. This book covers a wide range of topics related to car touring. See `http://www.reedmedia.net/books/family-road-trip/` for information.

1 Introduction

Hiking, camping, helping grandmothers cross the street, service projects, uniforms, doing a good turn daily, and being prepared. These are all common examples of Boy Scouting.

Boy Scouts are members of a scouting organization — for this book — the Boy Scouts of America (BSA). This program is for boys who are 11 years old to 18 years old — or beginning at 10 years old for boys who have earned the Cub Scout Arrow of Light award or have completed the fifth grade. Boy Scouts of America also encompasses the Tiger Cubs and Cub Scout programs for younger boys, Varsity, and Venturing which also includes co-ed young adults. (This book doesn't cover these younger or older scouting programs.)

Scouting emphasizes outdoor activities, camping, physical fitness, lifelong learning, trying new skills, safety, service, responsibility, and leadership. According to the Boy Scouts of America website, it "provides a program for young people that builds character, trains them in the responsibilities of participating citizenship, and develops personal fitness."

Boy Scout units are organized into a large group of boys known as a *troop*. An individual troop is made of one or more smaller youth-led patrols.

The official mission statement of the Boy Scouts of America is: "to prepare young people to make ethical and moral choices over their lifetimes by instilling in them the values of the Scout Oath and Law." The official vision statement is: "The Boy Scouts of America will prepare every eligible youth in America to become a responsible, participating citizen and leader who is guided by the Scout Oath and Law."

The Scout Oath and Law

The Scout Oath (also known as the Boy Scout Promise) and the Scout Law share the promise and characteristics that the boy agrees to live by. The Scout Oath is:

> On my honor I will do my best
>
> To do my duty to God and my country
>
> and to obey the Scout Law;
>
> To help other people at all times;
>
> To keep myself physically strong,
>
> mentally awake,
>
> and morally straight.

The following is the Scout Law:

> A Scout is: Trustworthy, Loyal, Helpful, Friendly, Courteous, Kind, Obedient, Cheerful, Thrifty, Brave, Clean, [and] Reverent.

This is the honor code that scouts live by. They agree to follow this to join Boy Scouts and they reaffirm that they follow this daily to pass each of their rank advancements.

Numerous activities and awards related to these *aims of Scouting* — of developing character, citizenship, and mental and physical fitness — are provided by the Boy Scouts program. The highest advancement is the Eagle Scout rank which requires several prerequisite ranks — which must be earned in order — and many character-building citizenship and fitness activities. The BSA defines eight methods to meet the goals of scouting: ideals (such as the Oath and Law), Patrol Method, outdoor activities, rank advancement, adult association, personal growth, leadership development, and the uniform. These topics are covered throughout this book.

Chartering Organizations

Chartering organizations are groups that are offered a *charter* by their local Scout council to offer scouting programs to their local communities. The reasons that groups charter scouting units vary widely (e.g. The Church of Jesus Christ of Latter-Day Saints embeds scouting in their Primary and Young Men's programs — every young boy or young man is automatically registered as a member of the age-appropriate scouting program). But all share the ultimate aims of Scouting — that is to promote *character, citizenship, and fitness*. In many cases, these programs are tied to other youth programs, are used as recruiting outreach to the community, or may simply be sponsored by a group of parents wanting a place for their children to do scouting.

It is not an overstatement to say that the chartering organization owns its scouting units — they have ultimate approval of unit leaders, are to ensure the unit has a place to meet, and have total authority over scouting units they charter. Without a chartering organization, a unit cannot exist. A good chartering organization generally will engender good scouting units. (A toxic relationship between the chartering organization and its scouting units is a danger sign.)

The chartering organizations with the most units or boys are The Church of Jesus Christ of Latter-day Saints, United Methodist Church, Catholic Church, Lutheran Church, American Legion, Lions Club International, Rotary International, United Church of Christ, Episcopal Church, and Christian Church (Disciples of Christ). Various other community organizations charter scout units too.

The United Methodist Church says the Boy Scouting program provides "sound, proven ways to instill values of character, citizenship, and respect for others while developing a strong reverence to God, self respect and self reliance."

A statement from the National Catholic Committee on Scouting says "the Scout Oath and Law of the Boy Scouts of America embody values and morals that are solidly Christian, indeed Catholic. Doing one's best; helping others at all times; paying attention to moral, mental and physical well-being; and striving to grow in virtue are all essential parts of Scouting."

The American Legion says "[s]upporting Boy Scout activities is natural for Legionnaires, who draw upon their service-learned skills and experiences as veterans to help build character and positive traits in young Americans. Few other post activities generate more goodwill from the community."

Rotary International says "the principles and goals of both organizations are closely allied. Character-building; service to country, to others, and to self; teaching leadership skills; and becoming aware of the world around us — these are all incorporated into the programs and activities of each organization. The values expressed in Rotary International's Motto and the Four Way Test ["Is it the truth? Is it fair? Will it build goodwill and better friendships? Will it be beneficial to all concerned?"] greatly parallel those articulated in the Scout Oath, Law, motto, and slogan."

The Church of Jesus Christ of Latter-day Saints (LDS) says that the Boy Scouting organization recognizes that religious principles are an important part of life and encourages the growth of family values. "We desire all young men to strive to earn the Eagle Scout and Duty to God Awards. ... As youth work on these goals, they will develop skills and attributes that will lead them to the temple and prepare them for a lifetime of service to their families and the Lord."

The History of Scouting in America

The Scouting movement was started in England in 1908 by General Robert Baden-Powell, a military hero in the Boer War. He published some of his military theories in a book called *Aids to Scouting* and was surprised to find that the book was used by boys as a guide for outdoor activities. Concerned about the lack of direction for boys at that time, especially working-class boys, Baden-Powell began to think about forming a youth organization.

At about the same time in America, a writer and naturalist named Ernest Thompson Seton was working with boys in the Woodcraft Indians, an organization he founded in 1902. The Woodcraft Indians was formed to give boys in Seton's community of Greenwich, Connecticut something productive to do with their time. The organization gained fame when it was featured in a series of articles published in the Ladies Home Journal, a national magazine. Seton and Baden-Powell met in 1904 and shared their ideas about organizations for boys. Within a few years, Baden-Powell gathered his first group of boys on Brownsea Island, wrote *Scouting for Boys*, and began the Scouting movement. The program quickly spread throughout the United Kingdom and then to other countries around the world.

In 1910, a Chicago publisher named William Boyce founded Boy Scouts of America. According to legend, Boyce was lost on a foggy street in London and was aided by a Scout who then refused a tip, saying he was just doing his duty. Boyce was so impressed that he decided to form a branch of the Scouting organization in America. He attempted to merge the new BSA organization with many independent Scouting organizations across the U.S., including the Woodcraft Indians. Ernest Thompson Seton was the BSA's first Chief Scout and served from 1910-1915. Seton is responsible for many Native American elements that are found in the BSA program.

The BSA grew rapidly and soon became the largest youth organization in America. In 2010, BSA served 2.5 million boys in its Boy Scout and Cub Scout programs.

Cub Scouts

Cub Scouting is for younger boys, usually aged 7 to 11 years old. Cub Scouts is part of Boy Scouts of America, but has different organization, different leadership, different goals, and different achievements. Its program helps prepare boys for a more successful experience as a future Boy Scout. Cub Scouts in the oldest program — Webelos — may wear a Boy Scout uniform with blue shoulder loops and their Cub Scout patches. The Webelos badge introduces several of the requirements of the first Boy Scout badge.

A Cub Scout graduates into Boy Scouting when he is 11 years old or at least 10 years old and has completed 5th grade or earned the Arrow of Light (the highest rank in Cub Scouting). While the Cub Scout den and pack are led by adult leaders, Boy Scout patrol and troop meetings are planned and led by the youth, with adult supervision and guidance. Boy Scouting provides the older boy with more experience outside of the home and neighborhood (including overnight hikes and advanced camping adventures), greater responsibility for planning activities, developing more self-reliance, and learning democracy for making group decisions.

Another significant difference between younger Cub Scouts and Boy Scouts is that parents generally do not sign off any achievement or rank advancement requirements in Boy Scouts.

Boy Scouts can participate in Cub Scouting by serving as a Den Chief or working at Cub Scout day camps.

This book does not cover Cub Scouting in further detail.

Varsity Scouts

Varsity Scout teams are for boys ages 14 through 17. It is an official part of the Boy Scouts of America. The adult leader is called the Varsity Coach and the youth leader is the Varsity Captain. They wear the standard uniform and have a Varsity strip above the right pocket. They can earn Boy Scout merit badges and advancement, plus they also can work on high adventure programs and sports to earn a Varsity Letter, gold bars, and pins. The highest award in Varsity Scouts is the Denali Award. The Varsity program is commonly found in LDS-sponsored units where it matches the ages of their Teachers' quorum. Many recreation centers have also adopted Varsity Scouting. Often the boys and leaders may be dual registered in multiple units. Boys may enjoy the older-boy team programs more than the regular Boy Scouting structure.

This book does not cover Varsity Scouting specifically. Nevertheless, Varsity Scouts pursuing the Eagle can follow this book.

Venturing

Venturing is for young men and women under the age of 21 who are at least 14 years old or 13 years old and have completed the eighth grade. This Boy Scouts of America program focuses on youth development and is designed to meet the needs of older youth. Its goals include helping young adults make ethical choices, experience fun challenges and adventures, be a skilled resource for scouting groups, acquire skills, and offer leadership roles — all within a supporting environment. They may earn Venturing achievements, such as the Bronze, Gold, Silver, Ranger Award, Quartermaster Award, and other awards.

This book does not cover Venturing, but this book is useful for boys in Venturing who are also working on the Eagle.

Summary

- The Boy Scouts of America program helps develop character, citizenship, and mental and physical fitness.

- These aims are achieved using eight methods (covered throughout this book): ideals, patrols, outdoors, advancement, adult association, personal growth, leadership, and uniform.

- Boy Scouts of America was founded in 1910 and now over 2.5 million boys participate.

2 Getting Started

There are a variety of ways to find a Boy Scout troop to join. You may belong to a church or civic organization that sponsors a troop or you may have friends or relatives who are in a troop. Boys who are in the Cub Scout program may be invited to visit Boy Scout troops once they have reached the Webelos rank. (Often cubs think they can only go to the unit they always have gone to, but a closer or better fit may be found elsewhere.)

Word of mouth and boy-to-boy recruiting is another good way to find a troop. For families with no connection to the Boy Scout program, the Boy Scout Council that serves the area can provide a list of local troops. Another resource for finding a troop is the Boys Scouts of America national website, which has a search facility that provides contact information for all of the troops in a given area: `http://www.beAscout.org/`

Choosing which Boy Scout troop to join is a personal decision that should be based on the needs and preferences of an individual boy and his family. Each troop has a unique focus and personality. Finding a troop that's a good fit is one of the best ways to ensure that a boy will stay involved and enthusiastic about Boy Scouts. Troops may offer an open house event or provide a recruiting packet or brochure to help sell their troop.

Before deciding on a troop, it's a good idea for a boy and a parent or guardian to visit a few different troop meetings. At the meeting, the boy should be invited to participate in the scout activities while the adult meets with an adult leader to learn more about the troop program. These are some of the things to look for when visiting a Boy Scout troop:

- Are boys or adult leaders running the troop meeting? BSA is designed to be a boy-run program and this should be evident during troop meetings.

- Does the boy have any friends or acquaintances in the troop? Many boys will feel more comfortable if they already know some of the troop members.

- Is the time and location of the weekly troop meeting convenient?

- Does the meeting seem well-planned and are the scouts busy? Is there a feeling of enthusiasm among the scouts?

- Is the patrol method used? Scouts should be working in patrols during the meeting and adult leaders should be ready to talk about the importance of the patrol method in the troop.

- Are the scouts dressed in uniforms? The uniform reminds scouts that they are part of a team. By wearing a complete uniform, they show their commitment to the BSA program.

- Are there several leaders in uniform present during the meeting? Have the leaders completed BSA training?

- Does the troop have a calendar of scheduled activities that includes at least one camping trip or hike per month? Was the calendar planned by the youth leaders of the troop?

- Does the troop attend summer camp as a group? Attending a long-term Boy Scout camp is an experience that a boy will never forget. It will help him gain independence and build friendships with other boys in the troop.

- Is there a New Scout patrol? Is there a youth Troop Guide and an adult Assistant Scoutmaster to help new scouts get started?

- Is there a good mix of ages and ranks among the troop membership? A troop with older boys has a better chance at being boy-run, but there should also be enough younger scouts to make a new scout feel comfortable and to guarantee the future of the troop.

- Does the troop have a program for older scouts? A High Adventure program that includes challenging hikes and other outdoor adventures will keep older boys engaged in Scouting.

A parent or guardian who accompanies a boy to a troop meeting should expect to hear about troop dues, fees, fundraisers and communication. The level of parent involvement should be explained. Some troops require adults to register as leaders and be involved, while others welcome involvement on a volunteer basis.

Finally, both boy and adult should be made to feel welcome in the troop.

Parents may want to consider why they want their son to join Boy Scouts. Kids are smarter than we give them credit for. If the parents want free babysitting, they get some of that, but the kids won't really enjoy the program. If they want their boy to become the "Youngest Eagle Scout" ever, that's also not a great reason for their son to join. If they want their son to learn to be a well-rounded, nice young man with leadership skills, that is a good reason to join.

All boys should be treated and regarded the same, including opportunities for participation and advancement. The BSA offers alternative requirements and merit badges for boys with disabilities or other special needs. Each council should have a special needs coordinator or committee that units can consult for details.

Registration

Once a boy has been invited to join a Boy Scout troop, the troop's Scoutmaster or Committee Chair will ask the parents or guardian to fill out an Application for Youth Membership. This form is provided by the BSA National Council and is the same for all youth members. A health history form should also be filled out. The troop's leaders need to know each scout's health issues in order to do everything possible to guard the safety and well-being of each boy.

When the youth membership form is turned in, the BSA registration fee should be paid. The standard fee is currently $15 per year. This fee may be covered by a troop's charter organization or individual scouts may be responsible for their fee. Some units may have a higher registration fee to suit their needs (such as $75). Each scout is also encouraged to pay an additional $12 for a subscription to Boys' Life magazine. Units may include this subscription in their annual registration fee. Boys' Life is the official monthly BSA magazine for youth. It's a great information resource as well as a source of entertainment for youth. (There may be a two to three month delay before receiving the magazine. Address changes should go directly to the magazine.)

Once a scout is registered in a troop, he will remain registered until he reaches the age of 18 or resigns from scouts. The troop will re-register each scout annually by completing a process called recharter. During recharter, BSA fees are collected from families and the troop roster is updated for the coming year. The registration and rechartering paperwork is usually handled by a member of the troop committee or by a volunteer parent from the troop. (Later fees and dues are introduced on page 43.)

First Steps

The following are suggestions for tasks to do when getting started with Scouts.

First Steps for the Boy

- ☐ Meet the Scoutmaster and Assistant Scoutmaster(s).

- ☐ Turn in the application and pay registration fees, if required.

- ☐ Find out what Patrol the boy is a member of.

- ☐ Meet the youth leaders, such as Senior Patrol Leader and Patrol Leader(s).

- ☐ Obtain a Boy Scout uniform with proper patches and accessories.

- ☐ Obtain the *Boy Scout Handbook*.

- ☐ Make a notebook or file folder to keep track of advancements.

- ☐ Make or obtain a calendar or schedule for upcoming activities and attend the meetings and events.

- ☐ Complete the requirements for the Scout badge.

- ☐ Review the requirements and plan for the achievements of the Tenderfoot, Second Class, and First Class ranks.

- ☐ Review the list of Eagle-required merit badges.

First Steps for the Parent

- ☐ Meet the Scoutmaster and Assistant Scoutmaster(s).

- ☐ Make sure the boy's application is turned in and registration fees are paid (if required).

☐ Find out what Patrol your boy is a member of.

☐ Find out who the youth leaders are, such as Senior Patrol Leader and Patrol Leader(s).

☐ Obtain a Boy Scout uniform with proper patches and accessories for the boy.

☐ Obtain a *Boy Scout Handbook* for the boy.

☐ Read and discuss *"How to Protect Your Children from Child Abuse: A Parent's Guide"* pamphlet with your boy.

☐ Help make a notebook or file folder to keep track of advancements.

☐ Make or obtain a calendar or schedule for upcoming activities.

☐ Encourage the boy to quickly complete the Scout badge requirements.

☐ Review the requirements and check that the boy has a plan for the achievements of the Tenderfoot, Second Class, and First Class ranks.

☐ Review the list of Eagle-required merit badges.

☐ Find out about parent volunteering opportunities and attend scout committee meetings.

First Steps for the Adult Volunteer Leader

☐ Meet the Scoutmaster, Assistant Scoutmaster(s), and Committee Chairman.

☐ Take the Youth Protection Training.

☐ Turn in the Adult Application and pay the registration fee.

☐ Find out who the youth leaders are, such as Senior Patrol Leader and Patrol Leader(s).

☐ Obtain a Boy Scout uniform with proper patches and accessories for the adult leader.

☐ Make or obtain a calendar or schedule for upcoming activities.

☐ Review and learn the basic requirements for the scouting ranks.

☐ Review the list of Eagle-required merit badges.

☐ Attend local Roundtable meetings.

☐ Attend local training opportunities.

These topics are covered in detail throughout this book.

Troops may have other steps in getting started, such as: taking a photo, turning in medical form, paying summer camp deposit, completing troop resource survey and other information forms, troop software registration, and joining mailing lists. Troops may also provide a *welcome* notebook, parent's guide, troop handbook, hat, neckerchief, and/or a custom t-shirt. They may also expect parents to be involved as chaperones or drivers.

Summary

- Choosing a troop to join is a personal decision with several things to consider, such as: youth should run the meetings, wear uniforms, attend summer camp, have programs for younger and older scouts, etc.

- Registration involves submitting a membership application, personal health history, and a nominal fee.

- New scouts should obtain a uniform and handbook and meet with scoutmasters and youth leaders for orientation.

3 The Patrol Method

The Patrol Method is not just one method of scouting, it is the only method. — Sir Robert Baden-Powell

A scout troop is split up into one or more patrols. The patrols are groups of scouts of around eight boys. They may be of similar age or advancement or they may be a mix of various ages and experience levels. They will do patrol activities and camp together. As a patrol, the boys assemble, play games, cook, eat, and travel together.

The patrol (and the troop) meetings are planned and led by the boys — with guidance and counsel from their adult leaders (who encourage and mentor behind the scenes). The older or higher ranked youth teach the younger or less experienced youth — this is a cycle of youth-led training and leadership. The patrol is self-governing.

This is the *Patrol Method*. It teaches youth responsibility and provides leadership experience. It may be difficult to implement, but it is important so the youth can learn how to organize, lead and teach. Some units hold patrol meetings at their own times and locations; other units hold patrol meetings at a set-aside time during the troop meeting. Patrols may have competitions with other patrols or do activities with just their own patrol.

Patrols have a descriptive name, yell, and flag. These identify the patrols and help build patrol spirit. The BSA offers over 35 patrol patches or the patrol may choose their own custom name and patch that the members wear on their uniforms.

Young or beginning scouts may start in the New Scout Patrol which emphasizes the first few ranks. They phase into a regular patrol after three to six months.[1] Some troops have an Older Scout Patrol (formerly known as the Venture Patrol not to be confused with the Venturing Crew) for experienced scouts ages 13 through 17. This veteran patrol may have an emphasis on more high adventure activities.

Scout Positions of Responsibility

The troop and patrols provide a variety of jobs for the boys to learn and lead. Young or new scouts can begin with easier tasks, while experienced scouts may have more advanced roles. There are no official BSA rules on age or rank for holding a position. Responsibilities may increase as the Boy Scout *grows*. A position of responsibility is a requirement for the final three rank advancements. Positions can vary by troop but typically last six months. Assignments are usually picked by the Patrol Leader and Assistant Patrol Leader with Scoutmaster approval. The scout should ask his Patrol Leader for a position if he doesn't have one. The boy should keep a log recording the dates he served in positions of responsibility. The common positions follow:

Senior Patrol Leader (SPL)

The Senior Patrol Leader is the head youth leader and commonly runs all troop meetings and activities. With the counsel of the Scoutmaster, the *SPL* may assign other youth leadership positions. He is also the chairman of the Patrol Leaders' Coun-

---

[1]LDS troops have an 11-year-old group with its members staying in it for a year. They generally do not participate in the weekly troop meetings.

cil (PLC). The SPL, PLC, and Scoutmaster work together to plan troop activities and programs.

The SPL is usually elected to his position by the scouts in the troop.[2] During the time as an SPL, the scout is generally not a member of a patrol.

Assistant Senior Patrol Leader (ASPL)

The ASPL is the SPL's assistant. He is appointed to his position by the SPL (with Scoutmaster approval). When the SPL is absent from a meeting or activity, the ASPL will take his place. The ASPL may be assigned to work with specific youth leaders, patrols, or projects. The ASPL is also not a member of a specific patrol.

Patrol Leader(s)

Every patrol has a Patrol Leader who helps plan and lead patrol meetings, keeps patrol members informed about activities, and delegates patrol duties. Members of each patrol in the troop vote for their Patrol Leader, usually for six months. The Patrol Leader represents the patrol at PLC meetings. The Patrol Leader may appoint an Assistant Patrol Leader.

The Patrol Leader should be considered the most important position — since the patrol is the fundamental unit of scouting.

Troop Guide

The Troop Guide mentors new scouts during their first year in Boy Scouts. He is usually an older scout and should have attained the rank of First Class or higher. He works with the

---

[2]In LDS troops, the SPL is commonly nominated by his Bishopric and sustained by his troop to constitute election.

Patrol Leader of the New Scout Patrol and provides instruction in the scout skills that are required for rank advancement.

Quartermaster

The Quartermaster is responsible for troop supplies and equipment. He helps make sure each patrol has the equipment it needs and that they keep the gear clean and in good repair. The Quartermaster often works with an Assistant Scoutmaster or committee member who helps purchase, maintain, and store the troop's camping equipment. Patrols may also have quartermasters too.

Scribe

The Scribe is the troop's secretary. He is responsible for recording decisions made at PLC meetings (but is not a voting member). He also takes attendance at troop meetings. In some troops, the Scribe collects dues from scouts or works with an adult committee member to maintain scout advancement records. There may also be a Scribe at the patrol level.

Historian

The Historian collects and maintains items that are related to the history of the troop, including photographs, awards, ribbons, flags, and other mementos. If the Historian is computer savvy, he may be asked to put together slide shows for troop meetings and special events.

Librarian

The Librarian maintains the troop's collection of reference materials, including merit badge books, regional maps, and guidebooks. In some troops, the Librarian also provides the merit badge counselor lists. Scouts check out materials with the Librarian, who also makes sure the materials are returned. The Librarian may also be responsible to track needed materials and propose acquisitions.

Instructor

An Instructor is an older scout who has mastered the skills required to earn the ranks leading up to First Class, including first aid, camping, backpacking, knots, and lashing. He leads skills demonstrations and training events. A troop may have more than one scout in the role of Instructor.

Chaplain's Aide

The Chaplain's Aide works with the troop's adult Chaplain to promote the BSA religious awards program.[3] The Chaplain's Aide may also lead the troop in benedictions and in saying grace before meals.

Den Chief

The Den Chief plays an important role in teaching Cub Scouts about the Boy Scout program. Often recommended to be an older scout, he works with a den of Cub Scouts as an assistant to the adult den leader. He helps with games, songs and stunts and is a friend and role model to the Cub Scouts. A Webelos Den Chief can also introduce the Cub Scouts to his Boy Scout troop.

---

[3]See page 85 about religious emblems.

Junior Assistant Scoutmaster

The Junior Assistant Scoutmaster (JASM) is an experienced 16-year-old or 17-year-old appointed by the Scoutmaster or by the SPL with the Scoutmaster's advice to help support and supervise other boy leaders in the troop.

Leave No Trace Trainer

The Leave No Trace trainer helps the troop follow the principles of *Leave No Trace*. Preferably, he should have completed this training and he may assist his troop members earn the Leave No Trace award. (For more information, see page 81.)

Order of the Arrow Troop Representative

The Order of the Arrow troop representative is a liaison between the troop and the Order of the Arrow (OA) Lodge or Chapter. He coordinates OA elections and promotes OA, service projects, camping, and leadership training. He reports to an ASPL.

Troop Webmaster

The webmaster helps maintain (and maybe build) the troop's website. He may keep it updated with photos and new content about past activities and upcoming schedules. He may work with the Troop Historian.

Bugler

The Bugler plays the bugle at ceremonies or to announce some daily routines of camp, such as reveille ("wake up"), retreat (at flag lowering ceremony), and taps (at end of the day). For the Eagle requirement, this is not a position of responsibility.

Cheermaster

The Cheermaster leads patrol yells, skits, and songs during activities and campfire programs. He does not direct the meetings though, just some entertainment. This is not an official position of responsibility (as defined for some rank requirements).

Grubmaster

The Grubmaster assists his patrol in planning menus and food arrangements. This is not an official position of responsibility (as defined for some rank requirements). It often helps scouts fulfill requirements for Second Class, First Class, and merit badges.

Firemaster

The Firemaster is the boy who sets up the axe yard and is in charge of the wood, fires, and setting up stoves, etc. He provides instructions in fire building and makes sure that campfires are safe. This also is not an official position of responsibility, but when approved by the Scoutmaster it can count for rank advancement in Star and Life ranks.

Training for Youth

Training should begin soon after new positions are assigned or elected. Training is important for the boys to understand and achieve their responsibilities and to know how to lead so they don't become discouraged. The Senior Patrol Leader, Patrol Leader, or other experienced scout should provide a quick introduction. The Scoutmaster or Patrol advisors may also help provide training. Generally a Scoutmaster would provide initial training for the SPL, the SPL would train the Patrol Leader, and the Patrol Leader would train the members in his patrol. Formal youth troop leadership training (TLT) should be offered to all current and potential youth leaders at least annually. Youth leader training is available for all leadership positions. The training for most positions is generic. Boys may wear a "Trained" patch after completing official training.

Often scouts are assigned a position, but never provided with a description of the position, specific tasks, or objectives. Months may go by without any training or explanation — this is a mistake. If your boy has a position, make sure he knows what his responsibilities are.

Many scouting requirements involve teaching other boys; the standard process is called EDGE, for: explain, demonstrate, guide, and enable. Tips for being a good leader follow:

- Showing examples of proper behavior and actions.

- Delegate work instead of handling all tasks alone.

- Don't give too many orders.

- Break down big jobs into smaller tasks.

- Allow others to share suggestions.

- Listen closely; ask questions.

- Complete leadership training.

- Learn skills before teaching them.

- Keep notes; write plans.

- Criticize politely, maybe in private.

- Respect others.

- Don't linger or waste time.

Official BSA books for Senior Patrol Leaders, Patrol Leaders, Den Chiefs, and other junior leaders are available. Additional training opportunities include SPL training at camps, overnight leadership retreats, mini-trainings as part of the Patrol Leader's Council meetings, National Youth Leadership Training (via the council), and the National Advanced Youth Leadership Experience (NAYLE).

The Patrol Leaders' Council (PLC)

The Patrol Leaders' Council is a planning meeting for the Scoutmaster and the troop's youth leaders. Like a *board of directors*, it includes at a minimum the SPL, ASPL, Patrol Leaders and Troop Guides. Some troops also invite the Scribe (to take minutes), Quartermaster, Historian, Instructors, and other youth leaders to PLC meetings as needed.

A PLC will typically take place once a month and is held outside of a troop meeting. It is conducted by the SPL and may last for 1 to 2 hours. Details for the troop program for the upcoming month are planned, including both troop meetings and the month's outdoor activity. The patrols can brainstorm ideas ahead of time — their patrol leaders represent these ideas at the PLC meetings. The PLC may take place at the normal troop meeting location or it may be held at the home of one of the scouts or the Scoutmaster.

The Scoutmaster is an advisor to the PLC. His role is to listen and provide guidance when needed. The plans and calendars that are made at PLC meetings should be subject to the final approval of the troop's adult leadership, including the Scoutmaster and the troop committee.

If your troop doesn't frequently hold PLC meetings, do encourage it.

Planning Conference

In addition, the youth leaders should hold an annual or semi-annual planning conference. This may be a full-day event, such as 9 a.m. to 4 p.m. with a lunch break. This important PLC meeting creates a calendar for the entire year, while the monthly meetings focus on specific details. The PLC focuses on goals, significant activities, and meeting themes while developing the yearly schedule. The troop committee reviews the program based on the *Guide to Safe Scouting* and realities of budget planning.

Summary

- Troops and patrol meetings and activities are planned and led by youth leaders.
- This Patrol Method teaches youth responsibility and provides leadership experience.
- Youth training is available for the numerous positions of responsibility.

4 Adult Leadership

The Boy Scout troop is run by the boys. Nevertheless, adults are needed for logistics, such as driving to campouts or paying for a safe meeting location, signing off or approving advancement requirements, supervision, and guidance. Adults should give the boys a chance to lead and not jump in immediately, unless safety is involved. The boy's association with positive role models is one of the key methods of scouting.

The chartering organization provides adult leaders and encourages adult leadership training. Often these leaders volunteer on their own, but in many cases, they are volunteered (or assigned) to a position. Local scout leaders are not financially compensated,[1] but scouting shouldn't be a financial burden either — so the unit or its boys should help pay for their activities, equipment, and travel. (Information about finances is on page 43.)

Some chartering organizations may have different processes for volunteers. For example, in LDS chartered units, the local church leadership asks members from their congregation to serve in roles for their troop. Their terms usually last for 18 months to four years, but the length is undefined. Generally in LDS units, adults do not actively seek out or cannot request these positions; nevertheless, parents can still volunteer to participate in their troop committee or as adult chaperones or merit badge counselors.

---

[1]The BSA may have local offices, stores, and camps with paid staffs. These are professional scouters.

Standard adult leadership positions include commissioners, local unit committee members, the Scoutmaster, and Assistant Scoutmaster(s). Many other volunteer opportunities are available too. The minimum age for adult leaders is 21 years old, except Assistant Scoutmasters who must be at least 18 years old. Approved adult scout members are known as Scouters.

The geographic area is organized into a large council which may include numerous units. The Boy Scouts of America has over 300 councils and over 150,000 units. The council usually provides a scout store, adult training opportunities, and organization for its local units — often led by professional scouters and non-paid volunteers. The council handles unit registrations, local marketing, and merit badge counselor registrations. Councils are often divided up into smaller districts. Districts provide localized training and assistance. (This book doesn't introduce the higher level national, regional, and area organizations.)

The webpage at `http://www.scouting.org/localcouncillocator.aspx` may be used to find your local council. The local council may also have a website that can be searched for the council's districts map, contact information, and calendar. (Note that your local unit may not meet in your district's boundaries, due to the address of registration or former meeting places.) You can also use the Wikipedia website (`http://www.wikipedia.org/`) to find councils by state and their districts. Also check your local phone books for Boy Scouts of America.

Commissioners

Commissioners are often knowlegdable area leaders who help local units by providing coaching and consulting for the unit's adult leaders. The Unit Commissioner is the representative for a unit (but not from the unit) and works with the chartering organization to assist with unit organization, yearly renewals, and sharing information.

Troop Committee

The committee members are parents and other adults who help with the troop, including rechartering (annual re-registration of the unit, leaders, and youth) and running Board of Reviews to evaluate the boys' advancement. These adults are also officially registered every year. It is often recommended that a representative from each scout's family participate on the committee.

Troops normally have committee meetings monthly which may last from one to two hours. They are led by a committee chairman. The typical agenda is covering upcoming events, planning (with focus on boys leading the troop with adults only providing counsel), money earning projects, logistics (drivers and chaperones for events), recruiting Scoutmaster or Assistant Scoutmasters, discussing scouting policies, meeting facilities, etc.

Commonly, the committee members may have assigned responsibilities and they share status reports. Committee positions include chairman, secretary, treasurer, advancements, outdoor activities, health and safety, service projects, enrollments, physical facilities, Board of Reviews, Order of the Arrow, patrol advisor, equipment, and other duties as needed. Or the committee may be informal and not have many or any positions. It is important that the adults do not do the boy's responsibilities, but provide guidance or assistance as needed. (For example, the committee member over equipment may assist the Quartermaster.)

Committees may have agendas available before the meetings and minutes provided later after the meeting. (Email may be used for committee discussions.) Some troops provide yearly plans (developed by the youth-led Patrol Leader Council) that the committee should review.

Note that some chartering organizations may have multiple

committees, such as separate committees for the Cub Scout program and the Venturing program.

A troop needs a strong committee to thrive. In addition, some units have a separate parents' auxiliary or ladies' auxiliary which provides different or similar support roles.

Scoutmaster

The Scoutmaster is the head adult supervisor of the troop's boys. He is at least 21 years old. He is the role model and lead teacher for the youth. He okays projects, approves activities, and guides advancements. The Scoutmaster is a cross between an athletic coach and a school guidance counselor. He doesn't run the youth meetings, but provides assistance and guidance as needed for the youth leaders. The Scoutmaster usually stays in the background; his corrections and criticism can generally be done after meetings.

He also runs Scoutmaster Conferences to individually meet with boys to discuss goals, advancement, and likes and dislikes of their participation. He may meet in the family's home with the parents and boy to help explain the scouting program and about any concerns they may have. He also assigns boys to merit badge counselors. The Scoutmaster is defined as the "Unit Leader" on various paperwork and forms.

Parents and boys should find out the Scoutmaster's preferred method of communication, such as phone, text messaging, email, or in-person. They may encourage most communication to be handled by Patrol Leaders and the Senior Patrol Leader.

Assistant Scoutmaster(s)

One or more adult supervisors are also assigned as Assistant Scoutmasters (ASM) for specific duties or tasks, such as a Patrol Advisor. A common example is supervising the *New Scout*

Patrol or as the 11-year-old Scout Leader (in LDS troops) for counseling and guiding the youngest, beginning scouts. The Assistant Scoutmaster must be at least 18 years old. The Assistant Scoutmaster is commonly recruited by the troop committee (except in LDS units).

It is important to note that scout troops are run by the boys and the lessons are taught by the boys. Boy Scouting teaches leadership and the youth actually should plan, delegate, organize, and run their activities. For example, the 11-year-old scout meetings are led by a Patrol Leader and the lessons mostly taught by the older scouts (who already learned and participated previously when taught by their older peers) — and the 11-year-old Scout Leader provides counsel and assistance with these meetings and instruction. Every patrol does not need an adult advisor.

Two-deep Leadership and No One-on-one Contact

All trips and outings must be supervised by two adults — this is one BSA-registered leader and another adult (such as a parent of one of the scouts). One of the adults must be at least 21 years old. In some cases with proper planning, patrols may hold their own youth-only activities (such as service projects or day hikes) without adult supervision. Overnight activities must have two-deep adult supervision.

Regular unit meetings may be held with just a registered leader and multiple boys.[2] One-on-one contact between adults and youth is not allowed. Any meeting should be held in view of another adult and youth. A youth shall never be alone with an adult.

---

[2]Note that LDS units require an additional adult for meetings and classes too.

Official *Youth Protection Training* is required for all BSA registered volunteers every two years. They must submit the certificate with their registration (or rechartering) application (as discussed later in this chapter).

Some chartering organizations, such as the Roman Catholic and LDS churches, have more stringent policies (including additional background checks) that should be followed if you are registered with their units.

Adult Training

The Boy Scouts of America provides various guidelines and training opportunities, especially related to safety.

Because the adult leaders are often assigned volunteers, they may not have any background or knowledge of the scouting program. Even if they have years of scouting experience, there is still lots to learn. (Or if they really know a lot, they can assist as a trainer for other leaders.)

The area scouting organizations provide adult leadership training.

All adult leaders must complete Youth Protection Training which covers child abuse prevention policies. The policies include two-deep adult leadership, no one-on-one meetings, no youth and adult leader camping in same tent, no corporal punishment, and no hazing.

For official information on the Youth Protection training and policies, visit the "Youth Protection & Adult Leadership" webpage at http://www.scouting.org/scoutsource/ HealthandSafety/GSS/gss01.aspx and the Online Learning Center at http://www.myscouting.org/.

The 24-page booklet, "How to Protect Your Children From Child Abuse: A Parent's Guide", is included in the beginning of the Boy Scout Handbook (or as an e-book download from `http://old.scouting.org/pubs/ypt/pdf/46-015.pdf`). It discusses child abuse, preventing child abuse, and talking with youth about abuse. It also includes the Child's Bill of Rights, Youth Protection joining requirements, and example scenarios.

Getting trained is the best way to provide a great program. Additional standard adult training courses include:[3]

- Boy Scout Leader Fast Start training

- This Is Scouting

- Troop Committee Challenge

- Scoutmaster and Assistant Scoutmaster Leader Specific Training

- Introduction to Outdoor Leader Skills

Various advanced training opportunities are also available, including: council training conferences, Philmont Training Center, and Wood Badge (where adults practice the Patrol Method). Districts hold monthly *Roundtable* meetings attended by adult troop leaders, committee members, and unit commissioners for sharing program ideas, adult recognitions, communication exchange, and supplemental training.

Getting Involved

There are many opportunities for parents and other adults to assist with the Boy Scout troop. The first thing to do is to attend and participate at the adult committee meetings. Some units have a resource survey for parents to complete to let the unit know about skills or work that can be shared. Opportunities include:

---

[3]Basic training may become mandatory across the BSA within a few years.

- Driving to events[4]
- Chaperoning (extra adult) at activities
- Serving as a merit badge counselor
- Assist on the committee
- Handle paperwork
- Pick up advancements and awards
- Support the troop financially
- Lead money earning projects
- Welcome new families
- Assist with meeting place maintenance
- Assist with equipment repairs
- Maintain a uniform closet (to redistribute uniforms)
- Send out newsletters or mailers
- Coordinate special activities
- Provide refreshments
- Help keep track of budget and finances (treasurer)

Parents may want to observe troop meetings or participate at activities occasionally. Of course, they should motivate the boys and attend recognition ceremonies. Parents are also encouraged to take Youth Protection Training. It is important to note again that the boys plan and lead the troop — the parents are only there to support, not to direct.

Adult Application

Be sure to turn in an adult volunteer application. This is required to be an adult leader or a merit badge counselor.

---

[4]Seatbelts are needed. Drivers do not need to attend the activities.

The parts of the adult application include signing a disclosure and agreement form for the Boy Scouts of America to do background checks including criminal records, sex offender registries, inmate records, court records, Social Security number verification, etc. The adult applicant provides a required Social Security number, driver's license number, ethnic background, occupation and employer, previous residences, character reference contacts, and questions about character.

Youth protection training must be completed. Proof of completion of the Youth Protection Training must be attached to the application.

Adult Registration costs $15 per year. This includes a subscription to the *Scouting* magazine. The application may also be used to subscribe to the Boy's Life magazine at a discounted price.

The application can be downloaded from the Boy Scouts of America website or obtained from the local unit. (Note that some councils only accept original forms and not downloaded printouts.) The completed and signed form is submitted to the unit committee chairman.

The application must also be signed by the unit committee chairman and the representative for the charter organization. The committee and chartering organization has the responsibility to check references and other information on the application before sending it to the council. The council does the expensive criminal background check. Copies are retained for the local unit's and the chartered organization's records. A copy of the form is sent to the local council where it must be accepted. The scout executive or designee must approve all adult members.

Merit badge counselors need to turn in a separate adult volunteer application and a Merit Badge Counselor Information form. (No fee is required for volunteers who are only merit badge counselors.) Commonly they are registered as counselors after approval with the local district or council. (This is covered in more detail on page 67.)

The adult volunteer is renewed each year through the annual recharter process. (Changing positions does require a new application.) The safety protection training should be renewed every two years.

Summary

- Trained adults provide logistics, guidance, and supervision — but not direct leadership — for youth activities.

- One-on-one contact between adults and youth is not allowed and all trips and outings must be supervised by at least two adults.

- Official Youth Protection Training is required for all BSA registered volunteers every two years.

5 Meetings, Activities, and Administrivia

Scouting offers various meetings and activities. Meetings promote patrol spirit and keep scouts motivated. Meetings are a good time for scouts to learn and practice scout skills and work on the requirements leading to First Class. The meetings also provide the boys with the opportunity to exercise leadership and plan troop or patrol activities. This chapter introduces the common on-going events. Campouts, high adventure, and special events are covered in later chapters.

At scouting activities, a scout group's attention is often silently communicated with a "signs up". This is the official scout sign (right arm at 90 degree angle with three fingers up) held at front of a group; as others see it they quietly and quickly come to attention and also hold up the sign.

Patrol Meetings

Patrol meetings provide opportunities for small groups to do activities together and for more youth to practice leadership. Patrol meetings may be used for planning upcoming activities, such as making assignments for patrol members. The Patrol Leader directs the meeting and he or the assistant patrol leader may discuss advancements and provide a report from the PLC.

Many troops allocate time at troop meetings to also have a time specific for patrol meetings. (See the typical troop meeting in an upcoming section.) Troops may have the patrols meet on different nights or days, or even on Saturdays. Patrol meetings are usually held at least twice a month up to every week. The location may be provided by the sponsor or may be in the home of one the patrol members — or at other places.

Patrol Activities

Patrol activities may include day hikes, service projects, and even patrol campouts. These events should not conflict with troop activities and must be approved by the Scoutmaster. In some cases, patrols may have activities without adult supervision as long as they have Scoutmaster permission. Great things can happen when patrols are empowered with real youth leadership.

Various required merit badges offer opportunities for a patrol (or as an individual), such as:[1]

- Watching an AED demonstration at an emergency medical facility or by the American Red Cross.

- Attending a municipal, county or state court session.

- Attending a city or town council meeting.

- Attending a school board meeting.

- Working at a charitable organization.

- Touring a state capitol or the U.S. Capitol.

- Visiting a National Historic Landmark.

- Visiting a site on the National Register of Historic Places.

- Participating in a community agency's emergency drill.

---

[1]In a few cases, the scout should discuss the requirement with the merit badge counselor before doing an activity. Merit badges are introduced in chapter 8.

- Participating in an emergency mobilization exercise.

Commonly a patrol should have an additional activity, usually outdoors, at least once per month. Taking months off makes it difficult for boys to continually advance, especially if boys sometimes are absent due to other (non-Scout) activities.

Some troops take a lot of the summer off. In addition to summer camp or high adventure, the troop should still continue on advancements, service, and ongoing activities during the summer school break.

Service Projects

An important part of the Boy Scout program is service to the community. Boy Scout troops should schedule service projects as part of their annual planning (as introduced on page 26). They should also take on service projects that arise throughout the year. Examples of service projects include community cleanups, rehabilitation of public buildings or private homes, volunteering at a senior center, or conducting a food drive (such as the *Scouting for Food* program).

Preferably the work is for people outside of the troop, and, of course, without pay. Performing service is also a requirement for many ranks and merit badges. Through service projects, scouts learn that they can improve the lives of members of their community. They experience the feeling of satisfaction that comes with giving of themselves to others.

Troop Meetings

Troop meetings assemble all the patrols together and should be boy-run. The SPL is the overall leader of the meeting. He is assisted by the ASPL, Patrol Leaders, and Instructors.

Troop meetings are generally at the same time each week, unless the PLC cancels it due to another activity, such as a campout on the previous or upcoming weekend. The meetings will typically follow this format:

Preopening

> This time may be used for meeting setup or it may include a game or activity for scouts to take part in as they arrive.

Opening

> Scouts line up by patrol for the opening flag ceremony. The Pledge of Allegiance and Scout Oath and Law are recited. Announcements, an opening prayer, or a uniform inspection may follow.

Skills Instructions

> Troop Instructors or other scouts demonstrate one or more skills. The instruction may be related to an upcoming activity. It should be hands-on and actively involve all the scouts.

Patrol Time

> Patrol Leaders meet with their patrols to discuss and plan upcoming activities. This may be the official patrol meeting.

Interpatrol Activity

> A game or skills competition lets the scouts burn off some energy. The competition is often tied to the skill that was demonstrated earlier.

Closing

> The scouts *circle up* and the Scoutmaster shares his thoughts about the meeting (the *Scoutmaster's Minute*). The SPL makes any final announcements. Scouts who have recently advanced in rank or earned

a merit badge are recognized. Most troops follow with some type of closing ceremony.

Post-meeting

Meeting cleanup. The Scoutmaster and PLC may meet briefly to discuss how the meeting went and plan for upcoming activities and the next meeting.

Commonly, the instruction, patrol, and activity time may be around 12 to 18 minutes each with the entire meeting from around one hour to 1.5 hours maximum. While there is a common format, troop meetings do not always need to be highly structured or rigid. The meetings should be begin on time, have a fast pace, and end on time. The meetings should have a specific purpose (such as preparing for a big event of the month), involve active participation, and provide variety.

Court of Honor

The Court of Honor is a formal event where the scouts' advancements and other progress is recognized. Family members, committee members, and members of the chartering (sponsor) organization are also invited. The Court of Honor is usually run by the Senior Patrol Leader. The rank advancements are often presented by the Scoutmaster or Assistant Scoutmaster assigned to the boys' patrol. Merit badges and other recognitions, in some troops, are awarded by the scouts' Patrol Leader or Senior Patrol Leader. The Court of Honor usually has a flag ceremony, short presentations from the boys, announcements, introductions of new members, and a Scoutmaster's Minute — the Scoutmaster shares an inspirational thought or brief lesson or story related to scouting. All scouts — including all leaders and most committee members — wear their complete Field Uniforms.

Normally, a Court of Honor is 30 minutes to 1 hour long, but may be longer for special events (such as a Veteran's Day presentation) or for many recognitions (like after a successful scout camp). The frequency of Court of Honors depends on the unit, but commonly it is held every two to four months. It is often held consistently to help scouts receive their recognition and to help encourage continued advancement. Note that patches and awards may be awarded soon after a boy earns them during a regular troop meeting, but then the boy can be recognized an additional time at the Court of Honor.

Communications

Scouting involves a lot of scheduling and needs a lot of sharing of planning information. Scouts and parents may need to know when things are due such as paperwork, forms, fees, and payments. A common problem is parents not knowing about upcoming activities, change of schedules, or needed purchases. Boys may forget to call patrol members about meeting changes. Often announcements at patrol meetings and troop meetings are not relayed to parents. Communication resources may be rarely updated.

Information may be communicated via:

- Announcements at patrol and troop meetings
- Announcements at Courts of Honor
- Posters at meeting place(s)
- Troop phone tree / phone lists
- Email list
- Print calendar for upcoming months
- Online calendar
- Troop newsletter

- Troop website
- Texting, Twitter, Facebook, etc.

Announcements may be presented by an adult leader or committee member, or done by a scout as a scout position (such as Webmaster). The sources of information, if applicable, should be frequently updated. The scouts should be encouraged to take notes when needed. When using a phone tree, they should report back to their leaders.

Adults and youth should not have any one-on-one private communication through social media, email, or other computer messaging. The communication should include other adults or be in a public forum.

Dues, Fees & Finances

Unit and per-scout expenses may include registration and re-chartering, books, uniforms, Boy's Life subscriptions, supplies, troop and patrol equipment, troop management software, insurance, campsite fees, troop flags, awards, camping and outdoor gear, trainings (for adults or youth), summer camp registrations, high adventure activities, travel, special events, and a lot more. Scouting is often expensive — or may be very inexpensive depending on the troop.

The treasurer (a committee member), the scribe, and the Scoutmaster prepare a draft budget which the PLC reviews and improves. Then the troop committee approves it and it is presented to the parent and boys.

Troops may have monthly or weekly dues; these are collected by the scribe and submitted to the treasurer. Troops may have annual activity or outing fees. Troops make keep financial accounting per boy versus for the whole troop. Some charter organizations cover the registration costs for the boys and financially support the troop for its activities. (They may even cover the costs of uniforms and books.) Often while some troops do not have dues or registration fees, they still may have costs for food for campouts and expenses for week-long camps, for example. A common amount for additional operational expenses may be $30 to $50 annually.

Some troops suggest for significant costs (like high adventure) that 1/3 comes from the troop's fundraising, 1/3 from the parents, and 1/3 from the boy himself (paid jobs, birthday gifts, allowance, etc).

Troops may have money earning projects, but must follow the policies of their chartering organization, their council, the BSA, and their local government. The BSA does not allow raffles. Uniforms may not be worn if selling commercial products or services (unless approved by the council).

In addition to earning funds for the troop, the local council also does fund raising, called *Friends of Scouting*. This helps support the council's management, program, and membership services. This may help fund summer and year-round scout camps, professional staff, training, providing insurance, and recognition of volunteers. Commonly, the Friends of Scouting seeks pledges of $175 to $10,000. As your family donates to scouting, you may want to understand whether your money is going to your local troop or to the council. The council and its districts are the only entities approved to solicit funds; units cannot solicit donations of money.

Summary

- Meetings are boy-run and may provide organized activities, skill instruction, and various formalities.

- Courts of Honor are formal events for families and the community to share in the recognition of the scouts' progress.

- Troops have financial costs that the boys and their families may be responsible to assist with.

6 The Uniform and Scout Supplies

Scouts and their leaders wear uniforms. They are an equalizer regardless of social or economic status and help build camaraderie. The standard uniform is BSA issued and includes the button up khaki shirt, green shorts or pants, and scout socks.

The Boy Scout uniform identifies each scout as a member of the Boy Scout organization. It unites the boys in a troop and shows they are part of a team. The uniform represents the history of the Scouting organization. It also recognizes each boy's individual accomplishments with patches and award pins.

The official Boy Scout uniform is referred to as the Field Uniform. It consists of a scout shirt, scout pants or shorts, a scout belt, scout socks and leather or canvas shoes or hiking boots. (Some official scout pants contain a built-in belt, so an extra belt is not needed.) The shirt is available with long or short sleeves. Many troops wrongly call this the Class A uniform, but the BSA organization always refers to it as the Field Uniform. The Field Uniform is worn for all formal occasions, including Courts of Honor and Boards of Review.

Most troops also have a custom t-shirt — maybe with a troop logo — that is worn with scout pants or shorts for campouts and other activities. BSA refers to this as the Activity Uniform, though many troops wrongly call it the Class B uniform. Each troop can decide whether the Field or Activity Uniform will be worn for troop meetings, patrol meetings, service projects, and other occasions.

BSA allows troops some flexibility in the details of the official uniform. For example, the scout neckerchief is optional. Each troop has the option of requiring scouts to wear an official BSA neckerchief or doing without the neckerchief altogether. Troops can also design and supply their own custom neckerchief. Another optional element is the scout hat. Some troops require that all scouts wear an official hat while others don't. A troop may also decide that each patrol will have its own neckerchief, t-shirt, and/or hat.

The boys should be encouraged to properly wear their uniforms. Many troops perform uniform checks at the start of meetings.

Buying a Scout Uniform

The family of each scout is responsible for the cost of his uniform. Often boys are encouraged to earn their own uniform. After the initial investment has been made, most boys are able to wear their uniform for several years. Many troops maintain a *uniform bank* that consists of uniforms that scouts have outgrown. When the cost of a scout uniform is a hardship and no secondhand uniforms are available, the troop, local council, or charter organization should be able to help purchase a scout's uniform or help him earn the money for a uniform.

Many units will allow the use of non-BSA branded pants and shorts so long as they are the appropriate color and not from military uniforms. Camouflage is absolutely prohibited.

The cost of a basic Boy Scout uniform, including shirt, convertible pants, belt, socks, hat and insignia, is currently about $110 - $130.

It is important to note that uniforms sometimes get damaged — they may get ripped, stained, or permanently soiled during outdoor or sporting events. You may want to encourage the use of lower-cost Activity Uniforms for active or dirty events.

Uniform Patches

Boy Scouts wear several patches (also known as *insignia*) on their uniforms. These patches identify a scout's troop and patrol, reinforcing the sense of being part of a team. The patches are purchased separately at the scout shop and sewn to the scout shirt. In addition to the standard uniform patches, each scout also wears green shoulder loops on the shoulder epaulets of his scout shirt.

The following are the standard patches that scouts wear and their location on the scout shirt. The Boy Scout Handbook includes charts on the inside of its front and back cover showing exactly how each patch is positioned.

Right Sleeve

- U.S. flag emblem is centered below the shoulder seam.

- Patrol patch is beneath the U.S. flag (may be supplied by the troop or purchased after the scout is assigned to a patrol).

- Quality Unit Award is beneath the patrol patch. This is an optional patch that is worn if the troop has earned this award.

Left Sleeve

- Council shoulder patch is centered below the shoulder seam.

- Veteran unit bar is worn by troops that have been chartered for more than 25 years. The troop will provide information about this patch.

- Troop numerals are beneath the shoulder patch or veteran unit bar. These may be individual patches or a single, custom-ordered patch with the entire troop number.

- The scout's current leadership position patch is immediately below the troop number. (See chapter 3 for details.)

Right Pocket

- One temporary patch, such as a camporee patch, may be worn centered on the right pocket. (This may be sewn or hang from a loop or a plastic sleeve.)

- Members of the Order of the Arrow may wear a patch, representing their lodge, on the flap.

Left Pocket

- The World Crest emblem is worn centered above the left pocket, an equal distance between the top of the pocket and shoulder seam.

- The current rank patch (such as the First Class or Eagle Scout) is worn centered on the left pocket, below the flap.

- If the scout earned the Arrow of Light award as a Webelos Scout, the badge is worn below the left pocket.

- A commonly awarded *knot* is the religious emblem worn centered above the pocket flap. (See page 85.)

Additional patches are added to or changed on the shirt as the scout completes requirements, earns awards, and is assigned to leadership positions in the troop.

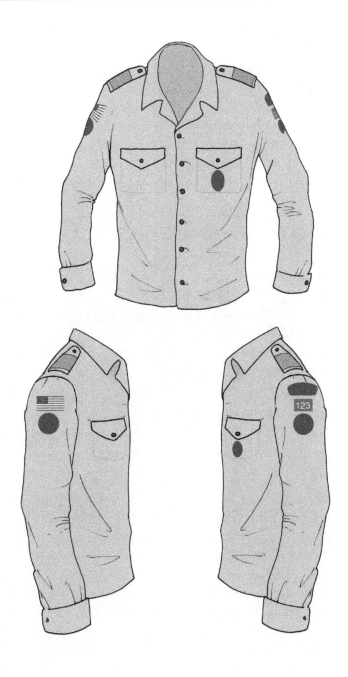

Merit Badges

The merit badges (small circle patches) are worn on a forest green merit badge sash that overlaps the right shoulder and crosses over to the left hip. These are sewed with even spacing three per row starting a half inch to a few inches from the top, working one row at a time down the front of the sash. Chronological is the normal procedure, but some attempt to sew them in groups or colors, such as the silver-bordered Eagle-required first or down the middle, which may require lots of resewing or extra planning. You may want to ask your troop if they have an optional theme for this.

The merit badge sash is generally not worn weekly, but for formal events. Many scouts place temporary patches (such as summer camp patches) on the back of the sash. Only merit badges go on the front of the sash. The sash is not worn draped over the belt. For shorter scouts, the sash may be folded and resewn at a seam to shorten it. The scout store may offer two lengths, such as 30 or 36 inches.

Scouts may also sew up to six merit badges on the outside bottom of the right sleeve (on long sleeve shirts); but this is not common. When seven merit badges have been earned, it is suggested to transfer them to a sash.

Sewing

Patches should be sewn on as soon as possible so the boy may be able to show his accomplishments and feel his success. It is also a good example for the other scouts. It is suggested that the patches be washed once in advance in hot water, because the glue holding the patch together may bleed onto a shirt. Remember that rank advancements (on the left pocket) and some other patches (such as the leadership position on the left sleeve) may be replaced periodically, so they should not be sewn on too permanently that they are hard to remove. Some use glue, *badge bond*, or other no-sew solutions to hold on patches, but this may be a bad idea for uniforms that may get lots of wear. Some fabric glues tend to stain the underlying shirt.

Sewing may be done by hand or with a machine — but in many cases, like on pocket, it is difficult or near impossible to use a standard sewing machine. Often mothers sew patches on the uniform. Others may pay professionals to put on patches too. It is a good idea to encourage or have the boys sew on their own badges.[1] Be sure that the patches are in the correct places and look neat.

Recent Changes to the Boy Scout Uniform

The Boy Scout uniform has undergone numerous changes in the past 100 years, including a 1980 makeover by fashion designer Oscar de la Renta that removed most of the uniform's resemblance to military uniforms. The next big change came in 2008 when the Centennial Boy Scout Uniform was introduced. The most noticeable difference in the Centennial Uniform is the change in color scheme. The old uniform's red shoulder loops and troop numerals are now green and the new cap is exclusively green.

Another big change in the Centennial Uniform is in the fabrics used. Traditional cotton shirts and poplin pants are still available, but scouts and Scouters also may choose a uniform made from modern outdoor-oriented fabrics, including nylon and microfiber. Scout socks are now available in a polyester and nylon blend that dries faster and wears longer than cotton or wool.

---

[1]The author sewed on his own patches starting as a eight-year-old Cub Scout.

Some of the other changes seen in the Centennial Uniform were made for utilitarian reasons. The shirt pockets are pleated so they can hold more, back pleats are provided for ease of movement, and buttons and tabs make it easier to roll up long sleeves. The new shirts also provide a pocket on the sleeve.

The Centennial Boy Scout Uniform was introduced on a transitional basis. This means that scouts can continue to wear older uniforms until they need to be replaced and they can combine pieces from old-style uniforms with new pieces.

Extras

Often scouts collect custom neckerchiefs, neckerchief slides (aka bolos), patches, hats, belt buckles, and other scout effects. They may wear vests and jackets adorned with various patches and pins earned or received by attending events. In fact, many are collectibles, and scouts often enjoy trading patches and other items.

Scout Books

In addition to the uniform, the scout should have his own official Boy Scout Handbook. Normally this would not be a used edition since it has checklists and up-to-date requirements that will be dated and signed. The handbook provides a plethora of information teaching many outdoor skills, citizenship, and other scouting standards. It often provides explanations and background on many of the scouting rank requirements. The BSA provides the book in both ring bound and perfect binding editions. Some scouts use a book sleeve or jacket to protect their handbook which may be taken on many activities. Scoutmasters often encourage scouts to bring their books to meetings so requirements can be signed off in it — or so its information can be compared with the troop's official charts.

Additional books include the *Boy Scout Requirements* book (covers requirements for ranks, merit badges, and other special opportunities), merit badge books, and handbooks for various youth leadership positions.

Buying Scout Supplies

Boy Scout uniforms, patches, and supplies can be purchased at an official BSA Scout Shop or a distributor of BSA merchandise. The BSA Scout Shop Locater website can be used to find all of the Scout shops and distributors in a specific area:

`http://www.scoutstuff.org/retail/store-locator`

In addition to uniforms, most Scout Shops also sell outdoor apparel, camping equipment, gifts, and a variety of other scout items including merit badge books and supplies. ScoutStuff.org is the official BSA online retail store. It sells the same items that are found in Scout Shops.

ScoutStuff.org can also be visited for free forms and documents, including uniform checklists, merchandise catalogs, and Scouting newsletters.

Other shops such as Christian bookstores and farm supply stores (especially in remote areas) may sell scouting uniform parts and books. (They don't sell advancement badges though.) Also, Goodwill or Salvation Army stores are often a great resource, especially for buying camping equipment and/or uniforms when boys are growing.

Summary

- The standard full Field Uniform is used for formal occasions.

- The troop also may have an Activity Uniform (such as a custom t-shirt and cap) which may be used for various activities.

- The Boy Scout Handbook, uniforms, and other supplies may be purchased from an official BSA Scout Shop or a distributor of BSA merchandise.

7 Rank Advancements

A boy may be a scout without advancing, but may miss out on the value of the experience. The Eagle Scout award is the highest rank in scouting. The Eagle Scout award requires that other ranks must be earned first and in order: Tenderfoot, Second Class, First Class, Star, and Life. The goals of the ranks include learning and performing new skills, outdoor and camping activities, teaching skills, community service, and leadership responsibilities. The Eagle rank and some of its prerequisite ranks also need merit badges earned — some are elective and some are required. Merit badges are awards for learning about and accomplishing tasks in specific topics, such as Chemistry, Cinematography, Citizenship in the Community, and Motorboating. Merit badges are introduced in Chapter 8.

Note: this book doesn't list the specific requirements for the many ranks and awards. Please see the official up-to-date Handbook, Requirements, and Merit Badge books for the exact requirements.

Scout Badge (Joining Requirements)

The Scout badge is normally the easiest and fastest award earned. In fact, Cub Scouts who received their Webelos Badge or Arrow of Light award already studied and learned many of the Scout rank requirements.

It is not a rank, but this badge is awarded to the newest scouts when they turn in the completed scouting application; say the

Pledge of Allegiance; show the Scout sign, show the Scout salute; demonstrate the Scout handshake (normal handshake but with the left hand); tie the square knot; agree to live by the Scout Oath (aka Promise), Scout Law, motto, slogan, and the Outdoor Code; describe the Scout badge; with a parent (or guardian) complete the *"How to Protect Your Children from Child Abuse: A Parent's Guide"* booklet exercises; and complete the Scoutmaster conference.

No merit badges are required for the Scout badge. Also there is no time requirement.

Signing Rank Requirements

The BSA program leaves several areas of Scouting to the discretion of each troop to manage. One of these is the question of who signs off rank requirements. Each scout must complete about 60 requirements (not including the numerous requirements for merit badges) to advance from Tenderfoot to Eagle. Working directly with every scout on each rank requirement is too big a job for many Scoutmasters, so the Scoutmaster and troop committee will usually decide who else can sign off the requirements. Only leaders, adult or youth (with approval), may sign off requirements. In most troops, any Assistant Scoutmaster can sign off requirements.

Troops may find that allowing older scouts to sign off rank requirements gives them an increased sense of responsibility and empowerment.

Anyone who signs off requirements should have a basic knowledge of the skill that they are signing off on. This may come from past experience or can be learned from another adult in the troop by reading the *Boy Scout Handbook* or in BSA training courses.

Advancements need to be the boy's responsibility and not the parents'. Parents can encourage their sons to work on advancements, help them learn and practice skills, and help them meet the right people to sign off advancements. The boys should obtain signatures, call to make appointments, etc.

A member of the adult committee — the advancement chair — usually keeps a record of the scout's advancement progress. The committee may provide a progress report listing your boy's achieved requirements for your records. They may use software to manage records (see page 96).

Ranks

The Scouting ranks are used to evaluate the boy's progress in scouting and are used to highlight and honor his accomplishments. The Boy Scout Handbook has many pages covering the rank requirements. Note this book does not include all the requirements (and they may have changed). Be sure to follow the recent Handbook or Requirements book for full details. The following sections introduce each of the ranks leading up to Eagle.

Tenderfoot

The Tenderfoot rank requirements include campout preparation, pitching a tent, camping overnight, knot tying and rope care, flag presentation, and first aid and safety skills. It also includes documenting and improving in some fitness exercises. No merit badges are required for the Tenderfoot rank. Tenderfoot doesn't have a time requirement — a new scout can earn this as fast as he can do all the requirements.

Second Class

No merit badges are required for the Second Class rank. Also there is no specific time requirement, but note that the required activities may take a couple months — two overnight campouts are required.

First Class

No merit badges are required for the First Class rank. As for the Second Class rank, there is no specific time requirement to earn the First Class, but note that the required activities may take a few months. The campouts and patrol activities done since joining Boy Scouts can be used towards the First Class activity requirement.

Star

The Star rank has time and merit badge requirements. The scout needs to actively serve in a position of responsibility for four months after earning the First Class. The scout needs to earn any four Eagle-required merit badges and two additional merit badges. The scout also does at least six hours of service projects — this needs to be approved by the Scoutmaster before starting.

Life

The Life rank requires six months of actively serving in a position of responsibility (after earning the Star rank), five more merit badges (three from the Eagle-required list), and participate in six more hours of Scoutmaster-approved service projects.

Eagle

The Eagle rank requires six months of actively serving in a position of responsibility as a Life scout and ten more merit badges of which five are from the Eagle-required list (for a minimum of 21 earned).

The main task of the Eagle rank is planning and leading a service project that benefits a non-profit organization other than Boy Scouting.

For details specifically for the Eagle rank, see Chapter 13.

Time Requirements

The time requirements for the Star, Life, and Eagle ranks begin (assuming continuous active participation) when the previous rank is earned — which is when the Board of Review requirement is completed. (It is not based on the date of recognition, because this may be an unwarranted delay.) The requirements for Tenderfoot through First Class can be earned simultaneously.

All requirements (for a single rank) other than the Eagle Board of Review must be completed before the scout's 18th birthday.

Advancement should not be a race, but rather a learning experience for a boy. Some boys will be highly motivated to advance and will race through the ranks, others will get to First Class, then take a break (sometimes until they are 17), other boys will stay in scouts until they are 18 and will never achieve Eagle — but in each case if scouting was done correctly, the boys will have acquired the character, citizenship, and fitness aims of scouting.

Troops may not force attendance rules, so active participation and demonstrating scout spirit may simply be done by being registered and being informed of unit activities on a regular basis. Nevertheless, you may find scoutmasters that are still very strict — even if the boy is busy with Order of the Arrow or working at scout camps, but not actively participating with his own troop, his Scoutmaster may not pass his time requirements. Be sure to discuss this with your Scoutmaster if attendance is a concern.

Scout Leadership Positions

In order to earn the ranks of Star, Life and Eagle, a scout must fulfill the duties of a leadership position or a position of responsibility in the troop. The official positions are listed on page 18.

In addition to the official positions, a Scoutmaster can assign a leadership project to a scout in order to satisfy the leadership requirements for the ranks of Star and Life.

Service Hours for Rank Advancement

Participation in service projects is part of Boy Scout rank advancement. Service hours are required for the following ranks:

- Second Class — 1 hour
- Star — 6 hours
- Life — 6 hours

Scouts may do this service as an individual or as part of a patrol or troop service project. It is not required for all the time to be done on the same project.

Many scouts complete their service hours by helping with an Eagle Service Project. In order to earn the rank of Eagle, a scout must plan and lead a service project that benefits a church, school or non-profit organization. Leadership is a key element of the Eagle Service Project. Instead of completing the project himself, the scout must provide leadership to others who are assisting with the project. (This is covered in detail in chapter 13.) Scouts who help with an Eagle project should get credit for service hours towards rank advancement.

Each troop should decide how to approve and track service hours. The scout should consider getting approval from the Scoutmaster beforehand. It may be up to each scout to keep track of his own service hours, or the troop may maintain a record of service hours.

Scoutmaster Conference

All ranks require a Scoutmaster conference. This is a short interview (usually ten to 15 minutes) with the scout and his leader to discuss scouting (and life) goals and likes and dislikes in scouting. The Scoutmaster may also review the scout's current rank requirements and ongoing progress at this time. The scout should make sure all his current requirements are completed as applicable before contacting his Scoutmaster to setup the conference appointment. The scout is not retested. While it is generally for rank advancements, it may be useful to hold Scoutmaster conferences for all boys every few months to discuss their progress. In some units, an Assistant Scoutmaster may do the conference.

Ask your Patrol Leader or Scoutmaster to discuss how to prepare for the Scoutmaster conference. Commonly, the Scoutmaster conference is done as part of an outing or during a troop meeting. Note that the interview is not private — the Scoutmaster must follow the no one-on-one contact policy (see page 31) by having the conference in a public place within view of other scouts and leaders.

Board of Review

Every rank (after the Scout badge) requires a Board of Review. This is similar to the Scoutmaster conference where a few adult committee members (who commonly are not involved with the weekly troop operations) interview the boy to also discuss the requirements, some of what the scout has learned, and how his participation in scouting is going. Note that the "Board" shouldn't retest the boys on the requirements. A Board of Review may also be held even when a scout is not ready for advancing yet and it is useful to evaluate the effectiveness of the unit.

The Scoutmaster, other unit leaders, and relatives do not participate in the Board of Review. Ask your Scoutmaster or Patrol Leader to find out your troop's preferred procedure for setting up the Board of Review. Many units have scheduled dates for doing Board of Reviews and others may do it on a case-by-case basis as requested by the boys or the Scoutmaster.

It is important that the scout always wear his full Field Uniform to the Board of Review. The Board of Review should be a formal event and helps the boy learn professionalism and job interview-like skills. At the Board of Review, the boy should introduce himself by name and state what rank he is completing, for example: "My name is John Doe and I am in the Flaming Arrows Patrol. I am a candidate for the Second Class rank."

The Board may ask the boy to recite or discuss the Scout Oath, Law, Motto, and Slogan[1] and demonstrate the handshake and salute. After the interview, the Board may request for the candidate to excuse himself for a few minutes while they "de-

---

[1]It is interesting to note, that while all the ranks require understanding and living by these standards, only the Tenderfoot requires reciting them verbatim. While not frequently done, the Outdoor Code might also be the subject at a Board of Review.

liberate" before calling the scout back in to tell them their decision.

The previous Scoutmaster conference can be used for practicing for the usually-more-formal Board of Review.

(The Eagle Scout Board of Review is introduced on page 135.)

Recognition

Well run units recognize a boy's achievement multiple times, including in the troop after completing the Scoutmaster conference and eligible for advancement, promptly after passing the Board of Review, and then the patch should soon be awarded in a troop ceremony (such as at the end of a troop meeting or at an outing). (The rank patch replaces the previous patch on the uniform's left pocket.)

It is good to recognize success soon after completing ranks or merit badges during the normal weekly meeting — instead of waiting for months for the next Court of Honor. This helps keep youth interested in scouting.

Formal recognition is done at the troop's Court of Honor in front of family, friends and the public. The boy may already have his patch sewn on by then so may only receive the award's card.

In some units, parents are invited to the front of the Court of Honor presentation and may also be rewarded with a rank advancement pin for the mother and/or a tie tack for the father. Some mothers may have a cloth necklace that contains all the pins for their son(s)'s ranks. Note that awarding the parents is not a rule.

Summary

- The rank advancements are achieved in order and some require positions of responsibility (or leadership positions), service hours, and have participation requirements.

- The Scoutmaster Conference is an individual meeting with the boy and the Scoutmaster to discuss his scouting progress, goals, and life.

- The Board of Review is a group interview to verify completed requirements and to encourage the scout.

8 Merit Badges

More than 120 different merit badges (listed at the end of this chapter) provide scouts the opportunity to develop or explore a talent or subject area. Working with knowledgeable counselors on individual merit badges, the scouts learn and apply new skills (or improve upon existing skills).

Small official books (or pamphlets) are available for every merit badge; they provide the requirements plus lots of supplementary information about the topic. Most of the merit badges are electives — scouts can choose what they want to learn and study. A core group of merit badges are required for advancement to Star, Life, and Eagle. This group of badges covers areas that are fundamental to the Scouting program, including citizenship, fitness, life management, and the outdoor experience.

Merit Badge Counselors

Scouts work with merit badge counselors to complete badge requirements. Merit badge counselors are adult hobbyists or professionals who have volunteered to offer their time and expertise to help scouts learn more about a specific topic. By working with an adult on a merit badge, a scout can experience personal growth and gain confidence.

Members of the community who register with Boy Scouts of America and complete BSA Youth Protection training can be a counselor. Registration for merit badge counselors is handled by the local council or district. A list of registered counselors in your area is supplied to troop leaders. Troops may also maintain their own merit badge counselors list or have a co-ordinator who recruits counselors for various merit badges. In some cases, the Scoutmaster, other adult leaders, or parents in the troop may be counselors (also if registered properly as a counselor).

There is no requirement on how many different counselors the scout must use. The scout can talk to his Scoutmaster to discuss that if it is a concern. It is common for a scout to have a few merit badges signed off by the same counselor.

Merit Badge Application

Generally the scout takes the initiative to start working on a merit badge of his choice and at his own schedule. Scouts can begin working on merit badges at any age or rank. Often scouts do not work on or earn any merit badges until they have earned their first few ranks.

When a scout is interested in completing a merit badge, he should ask his Scoutmaster or another troop leader for the name of a registered counselor for the badge. The Scoutmaster will provide a signed Application for Merit Badge, commonly a tri-fold perforated small blue card.

The Scoutmaster may also provide the names and the telephone numbers of a few approved merit badge counselors for the boy to choose from. (In some cases, the Scoutmaster may ask the scout to contact the district to get information about merit badge counselors.)

The "blue card" will be used by the counselor to keep track of the scout's progress — signing off each requirement on the card as it's completed. When completed, the merit badge counselor will sign the card multiple times and will keep one part for his or her records. The scout will keep one part for his records and the final part will submitted to the committee for the troop's records.

Note that some troops don't use the "blue card." Be sure to ask your Scoutmaster for the method used by your troop for the merit badge application.

Merit badges are awarded soon after signed off by the counselor at a regular troop meeting; and then the boy is later recognized at the next Court of Honor.

Working with Counselors

The scout will contact the counselor (usually by phone) to request to work on the merit badge, discuss what has already been done, to plan goals, and to schedule a meeting (or multiple meetings) with the counselor.

In keeping with the BSA Youth Protection buddy system, another person should always be present when a scout and merit badge counselor meet. This person can be a parent, guardian, relative, another Scout, a sibling, or a friend. Because of this, it is common for scouts to work on merit badges together.

At the initial meeting, the merit badge counselor and scout will review the merit badge requirements and agree on a schedule for completing the requirements. The number of meetings required to finish a badge will usually depend on the difficulty of the requirements and the abilities of the scout.

Some merit badges can be earned in a short time on a single day — others may take months to earn. Depending on the specific requirements, some steps do or do not require prior approval.

Merit Badge Requirements and Resources

Merit badge pamphlets (they're actually small books) are a valuable resource for scouts who are working on merit badges. The numerous books list the badge requirements and provides background information on the merit badge subject matter. Some counselors ask the scouts to read the official merit badge book but should only insist on the exact requirements to earn the merit badge.

Although scouts are not required to have a merit badge book in order to earn a badge, all the information needed to complete a badge is included in the book. Merit badge books can be purchased online or from a local Scout Shop for a small fee. Many troops maintain a library of merit badge books that scouts can check out and use while working on a merit badge. The Troop Librarian should be responsible for maintaining troop merit badge books. Another place to look for merit badge books is at the local public library.

The BSA book called *Boy Scout Requirements* also lists the requirements for all merit badges and for rank advancement. This is a handy resource for troop leaders and parents, but scouts should be encouraged to use the Boy Scout Handbook and individual merit badge books since they provide a wealth of information in addition to requirements.

Requirements are occasionally modified and updated, so it's a good idea to check online or in the *Boy Scout Requirements* book for the latest requirements. If a scout started a merit badge prior to a change in requirements, he has the choice to complete the previous version, or work on the current requirements. The most up-to-date merit badge requirements are listed online at Scouting.org:

http://www.scouting.org/scoutsource/BoyScouts/
AdvancementandAwards/MeritBadges.aspx

A useful website that provides numerous worksheets and thousands of links for additional information is the Merit Badge Research Center:

`http://www.meritbadge.org/`

Scouts and parents should be careful with other websites that list merit badge requirements since they may be out of date.

A number of activities may be used to complete requirements for multiple badges. But be sure to follow the requirements closely, as in some cases the tasks need to be done separately or with prior counselor permission. For example, at the time of this printing:

- Hiking merit badge hikes may not be used for different merit badges but may be used for Second Class and First Class requirements.

- The activities used for the Sports merit badge may not be used for other merit badges.

- The activities used for the Dog Care, Reptile and Amphibian Study, or other merit badges may not be used for the Pets merit badge.

- Stamp and coin collecting may not be done for the Collections merit badge — do the Stamp Collecting and Coin Collecting merit badges instead if desired.

Additional Opportunities

Scouts in most troops have a variety of opportunities to earn merit badges. They may offer merit badge classes as part of their normal troop meetings, but this may limit participation since some may have already earned it and some may simply not be interested.

When the troop attends a long-term summer camp, scouts can earn several badges over the course of a week. The local council may offer short-term campouts where scouts can earn merit badges. These typically take place over a weekend.

Another merit badge opportunity is a merit badge day, which is usually offered by a troop as a money earning project. For a small fee, a scout can sign up to attend a half-day or full-day of classes where he earns one or two merit badges. Merit badge sessions or clinics may also be offered by the local district or council. In many cases, these sessions are free of charge.

Many scouts earn their first merit badges at summer camp or at a merit badge day where easier badges (such as Fingerprinting, Art, Leatherwork, and Wood Carving) are usually offered.

To help more scouts within a troop earn merit badges, a merit badge counselor might offer a group session for a merit badge. In this case, BSA suggests that the ratio of scouts to counselor be no more than 8 to 1. A group of scouts will typically meet with one or two counselors to discuss requirements. Requirements are signed off for each scout after he demonstrates his understanding of the subject matter.

Local museums, historic sites, and learning centers may also offer merit badge programs. Search online or ask around to find out information for these opportunities too.

Eagle Required Merit Badges

The Eagle rank requires nine elective merit badges and 12 specific merit badges to be earned; for some an either/or choice is allowed. Starting with earning the Star rank, merit badges — including the Eagle required merit badges — need to be earned. (When the Life rank is earned, the scout will have at least seven required and eleven total merit badges completed.) The Eagle required merit badges are:

1. First Aid

2. Citizenship in the Community

3. Citizenship in the Nation

4. Citizenship in the World

5. Communications

6. Personal Fitness

7. Emergency Preparedness[1] — or — Lifesaving

8. Environmental Science

9. Personal Management

10. Swimming — or — Hiking — or — Cycling

11. Camping

12. Family Life

If more than one of an *either/or* requirements is earned, then the additional one(s) are counted as an elective(s).

The First Aid and Swimming merit badges have requirements that are linked to rank advancement. Many scouts earn these badges at their first Boy Scout summer camp or at a merit badge event. The Camping merit badge includes requirements that scouts earn during troop campouts (including camping for a total of 20 nights). Most scouts who are in a troop with an active camping and summer camp program can complete the Camping merit badge during their second or third year in Boy Scouts.

A portion of these badges are challenging and are often appropriate for older scouts. For example, Family Life, Personal Fitness, and Personal Management require the scout to set goals and track his progress over a period of several months. The three Citizenship badges (Community, Nation, and World)

---

[1]Note that the Emergency Preparedness merit badge requires the First Aid merit badge to be earned.

require a scout to understand government and his role as a citizen.

The Eagle-required badges teach life skills that a scout will carry with him into adulthood. A scout may gain the greatest benefit if he waits until he is more mature to work on the most challenging Eagle badges.

The Merit Badges

- American Business
- American Cultures
- American Heritage
- American Labor
- Animal Science
- Archaeology
- Archery
- Architecture
- Art
- Astronomy
- Athletics
- Automotive Maintenance
- Aviation
- Backpacking
- Basketry
- Bird Study
- Bugling
- Camping
- Canoeing
- Chemistry
- Cinematography
- Citizenship in the Community
- Citizenship in the Nation
- Citizenship in the World
- Climbing
- Coin Collecting
- Collections
- Communications
- Composite Materials
- Computers
- Cooking
- Crime Prevention
- Cycling
- Dentistry

- Disabilities Awareness
- Dog Care
- Drafting
- Electricity
- Electronics
- Emergency Preparedness
- Energy
- Engineering
- Entrepreneurship
- Environmental Science
- Family Life
- Farm Mechanics
- Fingerprinting
- Fire Safety
- First Aid
- Fish and Wildlife Management
- Fishing
- Fly Fishing
- Forestry
- Gardening
- Genealogy
- Geocaching
- Geology
- Golf
- Graphic Arts
- Hiking
- Home Repairs
- Horsemanship
- Indian Lore
- Insect Study
- Inventing
- Journalism
- Landscape Architecture
- Law
- Leatherwork
- Lifesaving
- Mammal Study
- Medicine
- Metalwork
- Model Design and Building
- Motorboating
- Music
- Nature
- Nuclear Science
- Oceanography
- Orienteering
- Painting
- Personal Fitness
- Personal Management
- Pets

- Photography
- Pioneering
- Plant Science
- Plumbing
- Pottery
- Public Health
- Public Speaking
- Pulp and Paper
- Radio
- Railroading
- Reading
- Reptile and Amphibian Study
- Rifle Shooting
- Robotics
- Rowing
- Safety
- Salesmanship
- Scholarship
- Scouting Heritage
- Sculpture
- Shotgun Shooting
- Skating
- Small-Boat Sailing
- Snow Sports
- Soil and Water Conservation
- Space Exploration
- Sports
- Stamp Collecting
- Surveying
- Swimming
- Textile
- Theater
- Traffic Safety
- Truck Transportation
- Veterinary Medicine
- Water Sports
- Weather
- Whitewater
- Wilderness Survival
- Wood Carving
- Woodwork

Summary

- Over 120 merit badges are available to learn new knowledge and apply new skills, such as Electronics, Plant Science, and Water Sports.

- The Eagle rank requires some specific merit badges to be earned.

- Merit badges are signed off by a registered counselor who is a hobbyist or professional in that area.

9 Other Awards, Achievements, and Recognitions

In addition to the numerous merit badges and the ranks advancements, scouting provides numerous other opportunities to learn and to have fun while providing special awards and recognitions for these efforts. These may be for the troop, patrol, or the individual scout — and some even for adult leaders. Several of these may be earned, while others are bestowed based on phenomenal service. This chapter discusses the most common of these extra opportunities and recognitions.

Note: This book does not list the requirements. See the official Boy Scouts Requirements book and other scouting applications for official requirements or contact the local council service center for applications.

Boardsailing BSA

The Boardsailing BSA patch (worn on swim shorts) recognizes scouts who can show skills with boardsailing preparation and sailing. The requirements also involve safety and explaining equipment.

BSA Lifeguard

Scouts, at least 15 years old, can become a BSA Lifeguard by completing the BSA Lifeguard course and American Red Cross

CPR/AED for the Professional Rescuer (or approved equivalent) training and numerous other tasks related to swimming experience, swimming skills, rescue techniques, search techniques, and advanced first aid. They also need to pass a written test and serve as a lifeguard.

Boy Scout Leader's Training Award

The Boy Scout Leader's Training Award is awarded for adults who completed training courses, served for two years, and participated or supervised in various activities, such as attending roundtables, Courts of Honor, and campouts.

Den Chief Service Award

Trained Den Chiefs may receive this recognition for serving in a Cub Scout pack for a year and various other requirements as listed in the *Den Chief Handbook*.

50-Miler Award

The 50-Miler Award may be earned for planning and completing a five-day 50-mile trail or boat trip (without motors) and performing service.

Firem'n Chit

The Firem'n Chit certification, available as a patch and a wallet card, covers fire safety, camp fire, and related Outdoor Code and Leave No Trace principles. In some cases, the card may be taken if the boy is not responsible with fire.

Historic Trails Award

Scouts who hike and camp for two days along one of 300-plus BSA-approved historic trails or sites may earn the Historic Trails Award. The scouts will also study the site and perform related service. Example sites include the Missions Historic Trail in San Antonio, Texas and the Covered Wagon Trail near Omaha, Nebraska.

Hornaday Awards

The William T. Hornaday Badge and Medals honor units and individuals for exceptional service or several years of commitment related to recycling, forestry management, pollution control, and natural resource conservation.

Interpreter Strip

The Interpreter Strip, which identifies a foreign language or signing, is worn above the the right pocket. To receive this, the individual shows he or she can translate (written and orally), write, and converse in the foreign language or in sign language.

Leave No Trace Achievement Award

Scouts who learn and live by the principles of *Leave No Trace* and perform related service and other requirements can earn this award.

A summary of the Leave No Trace principles follows:

- Plan and prepare before outdoor activities.

- Do activities on durable surfaces and be careful around and protect sensitive areas.

- Pack out litter and properly dispose of waste.

- Leave nature and cultural artifacts as you found them.

- Consider using stoves instead of campfires (and use safe and minimal impact decisions).

- Respect wildlife by observing from distance, not restricting water access, not polluting, and not feeding them.

- Be courteous to other outdoor visitors.

Your troop may have a Leave No Trace trainer (as listed on page 22).

Kayaking BSA

This patch, worn on swim shorts, recognizes scouts who can demonstrate knowledge and skill with kayaking.

Mile Swim BSA

The Mile Swim emblem is awarded to scouts who swim one mile over an approved and supervised course. The scout also discusses exercise and safety precautions and performs at least four days of supervised training.

National Camping Awards

Different level awards are available for troops for annual or cumulative camping, such as ten nights of camping annually or accumulating 1000 nights of camping. Individual scouts can also earn the awards (including family campouts).

National Quality Unit Award

The National Quality Unit Award recognized units that achieve certain goals during a charter year. These included adult leader training, two-deep leadership, six outdoor activities, on-time renewal, planning conference conducted, calendar published and presented at a family activity, service project, ongoing advancement, troop retention or growth, Boys' Life subscriptions, youth leadership training, and more.

The *Journey to Excellence* program also recognizes quality troops based on similar goals.

National Honor Patrol Award

The award may be earned for an entire patrol that shows three months success of performing as a patrol, such as good attendance, completing service projects (or "good turns"), advancements, and other requirements. This was formerly known as the Baden-Powell Patrol Award.

National Court of Honor Lifesaving and Meritous Action Awards

These awards recognize individuals for significant service or exceptional heroism — such as attempting to save a life with great risk. Since 1924, around 250 individuals have received the Honor Medal with Crossed Palms.

National Outdoor Badge(s)

The National Outdoor Badges recognize scouts accumulating experience in adventure, aquatics, camping, hiking, or riding. These five areas are available as segments that are placed around the embroidered National Outdoor Awards badge. The applicant must have earned his First Class rank and complete various related merit badges and additional tasks or awards.

The National Medal for Outdoor Achievement may be awarded to scouts who have earned multiple National Outdoor badges, merit badges, complete official Wilderness First Aid course, and perform other requirements.

Order of the Arrow

The Order of the Arrow (OA) is an honor society for scouting. It offers further leadership training and provides camp promotion. The candidate for OA must be at least a First Class and have 15 days and nights of camping within the previous two years. He is elected by his troop and approved by his Scoutmaster.

At a special event, such as a summer campfire program, the OA candidates are *tapped* out to begin the Ordeal process. This may involve camping overnight and spending a day in service — or hard labor. Often, the scout has little to eat, only a few supplies, and will be silent for the entire night and day. The other levels are the Brotherhood and the rare Vigil Honor.

An OA member is part of an OA lodge, often named after Native American terms. They may hold monthly meetings. OA members are identified by a lodge patch on their right chest pocket flap and a narrow white sash with a red arrow on it draped over the shoulder and opposite hip. (There are different sashes for each level.)

Paul Bunyan Woodsman

The Paul Bunyan Woodsman patch may be awarded for scouts who earn the Totin' Chip, teach Totin' Chip skills, and perform approved forestry service such as building a retaining wall or clearing trails with a three-quarter ax or saw.

Religious Emblems

The BSA believes that citizens have an obligation to God. Scouts have an on-going reminder to their duty to God and that a scout is reverent. Several religions expand on this for scouting and offer awards or recognitions for further study or following their faith's tenants. They define their own requirements which are approved by the Boy Scouts of America. For details or a specific booklet, contact your religious organization or your local council center. Common requirements may include: daily religious study, memorizing scripture verses, participating in worship services, reflecting on lessons learned, reaching personal goals, and performing service.

Often the presentation of the award is done during a religious ceremony. Scouts may wear a religious emblem square knot on their uniform above the left pocket.

Some troops participate in a special Scout Sabbath or Scout Sunday, commonly on the first or second week of February. They may wear full uniforms to their church service.

Scoutmaster's Key

The Scoutmaster's Key is an award for Scoutmasters who have already earned the Boy Scout Leader's Training Award and their unit earned the National Quality Unit Award twice (within three years). It requires three years service, additional training, and the Scoutmaster must conduct youth leader training.

SCOUTStrong Presidential Active Lifestyle Award

The SCOUTStrong PALA Challenge Award is a new recognition to encourage scouts and adults to live active lifestyles. To earn the patch, scouts need to keep track of 60 minutes of physical activity a day, five days a week, for six weeks. Adults need to do physical activity 30 minutes a day.

Scuba BSA

Scuba BSA is awarded to individuals who prove safety, knowledge, and swimming, scuba, and diving skills to an official instructor. This patch is worn on swim shorts.

Snorkeling BSA

The Snorkeling BSA award, which is worn on swim shorts, has numerous requirements including swimming, safety, survival, snorkeling signals, and various snorkeling skills.

Totin' Chip

The Totin' Chip is a contract scouts have to follow safety and respect guidelines with knifes, axes, saws, and other blades. The boy receives a card when he demonstrates the requirements to his leader. Often troops and scout camps require this before a boy may use blades (and it is a requirement for the Woodcarving merit badge). The boy may lose this privilege if he breaks the rules.

Trained Leader

The Trained Leader patch is awarded to adults or youth who have completed important standard training courses, including training specific to their position. The patch is worn on the left sleave below the position patch (that the training was for).

World Conservation Award

Scouts may earn the World Conservation Award by earning the Citizenship in the World, Environmental Science, and either the Fish and Wildlife Management or Soil and Water Conservation merit badges.

Knots

Some of these previous recognitions may be displayed as a square knot patch (or multiple patches) above the left pocket. Numerous knots are available for adults for personal achievement, recognitions, service, and training.

Summary

- Scouting rewards individuals for exceptional service and heroism.

- Many opportunities to learn and perform, beyond merit badges and rank advancements, are available for youth.

- Many of the awards are earned while others are bestowed.

10 Setting Goals and Keeping Track

As a boy begins in Boy Scouts, he quickly learns that responsibility for his advancement now rests on his shoulders. His parents and troop leaders are there to help, but he must learn how to set and achieve his own goals if he expects to advance and earn merit badges.

The Boy Scout program offers each boy the opportunity to set and work toward both short-term and long-term goals. The rank of Eagle is the final goal, but there are dozens of requirements and experiences that must be completed before a scout earns Eagle. Scouts should be encouraged to focus on the shorter-term goals that will eventually get them to Eagle — completing rank advancement, earning merit badges, and fulfilling leadership roles.

A challenge many adults and scouts find is that the boy is responsible for his own advancement. This means he has the responsibility of getting it signed off. Many boys will complete requirements but forget to get the check off.

A scout should advance at the pace that is best for him — this should not be a pace set too fast by his parents, or too slow by scout leaders.

Early Ranks

Beginning scouts — such as 11-year-old scouts or the New Scout Patrol — generally focus on earning the First Class rank.

Although the ranks of Tenderfoot, Second Class, and First Class must be earned in order, the requirements for these ranks can be worked on in any order. For example, a Tenderfoot Scout can work on First Class requirements, but he can't be awarded the rank of First Class until he has completed all of the Second Class requirements. Many scouts benefit from adult advice when it comes to prioritizing and planning requirement signoffs for advancement. It's recommended that each troop have one or more Assistant Scoutmasters who help scouts navigate the trail to First Class.

Many first-year scouts are eager to begin working on merit badges. A first-year scout should not be discouraged from earning merit badges, but his main focus should be on rank advancement. Working through the rank requirements for Tenderfoot, Second Class, and First Class will keep a new scout interested in the program and will teach him many important skills that he will be able to use on campouts, hikes, and other outdoor activities.

The National BSA organization encourages troops to advance new scouts to First Class within their first year. The following are some of the significant steps in the requirements for the first few ranks. (Be sure to follow the official and complete requirements.)

- ☐ Scout campout in a tent the boy helps pitch.

- ☐ Prepare and cook patrol meal at a patrol campout.

- ☐ Three overnight scout campouts.

- ☐ Attend ten scout activities (beyond regular meetings).

- ☐ For a campout, plan the patrol menu for three meals and serve as the patrol cook.

- ☐ Complete the BSA swimmer test. (See page 113.)

Once a scout has completed the requirements for First Class, he will begin to work on the rank of Star. This rank requires the scout to take on a leadership role that he may not be ready for. Spending a little more time on the requirements leading up to First Class will give the scout more time to mature and prepare for leadership.

As a scout progresses through rank advancement, he might want to start work on merit badges that are related to some of his special interests or hobbies. This should be encouraged since he is more likely to complete a badge when he's interested in the subject matter.

Keeping Interest in Scouting

Scouts who are slow to progress through the ranks may become frustrated and lose interest in scouting. They may need assistance in asking for help with requirements or in finding opportunities to earn merit badges. When a boy has adults in his life who show an interest in his progress and achievements in scouts, he's more likely to stay motivated. Troop leaders, committee members, parents, and guardians should work with scouts to identify their short- and long-term goals and help them plan how to achieve them.

Boys whose parents participate — such as joining the committee, becoming ASMs, working as merit badge counselors for more than just their sons, going on the occasional campout, driving scouts to summer camp, or even just attending meetings once in a while — not only enjoy scouts more, but do better in the program because they see that their parents are interested in them and the program.

Many boys retain an enthusiasm for Boy Scouts throughout their scouting career, while others go through periods of lethargy and may lose interest entirely. Some of the signs that a boy is losing interest in scouts include missed troop meetings and outings, a failure to advance, and a lack of connection with other scouts in the troop.

There are several possible reasons for scouts to lose interest. The first place to look is at the troop calendar. Does it include a variety of fun activities that appeal to all age groups? Because the Scouting program includes boys of many ages, it can be difficult to come up with outings that are fun for every age. One solution to this problem is to plan special opportunities for older scouts on a troop outing, or to plan some separate outings. For example, on a troop tailgate campout a group of older scouts might go rifle shooting or do some High Adventure activities like rock climbing or kayaking. Seeing older scouts participate in challenging activities will give younger scouts something to look forward to.

It's easy for a troop to get into a rut, putting the same activities on the calendar each year and returning to the same campsites again and again. Scouts don't always know about the opportunities available when they plan the troop calendar, so it's up to the Scoutmaster and other adult leaders to present them with new ideas. Roundtables, BSA training, and informal conversations with leaders from other troops are good resources for fresh ideas for troop activities and destinations.

If the troop program is not an issue, another reason for scouts losing interest is that they are overscheduled. Many families try to juggle sports, scouting, and other extracurricular activities — leaving boys feeling like they have no free time. If a boy complains of being too busy, it may be time to choose between activities and simplify his schedule.

When a scout is attending meetings and outings but seems to be stalled with rank advancement, he may need some help with setting priorities. Navigating through all the requirements leading up to First Class is not easy and scouts can get lost (especially in larger troops). If a scout is not advancing as quickly as most of his peers, a parent or troop leader can help him come up with a *to do* task list that will help him get back on track. For example, a scout may make a 3x5 card with task reminders and take it to his meetings.

If a scout really isn't clicking with the boys and leaders in his troop, it may be time to look for another troop. Switching troops may seem like an extreme measure, but it will allow the boy to give scouting one more chance before he drops out altogether.

Starting at Older Age

When a boy joins scouting at an older age, he still must do the ranks in order. Patrols may be based on locale, age, or rank — so talk to your Scoutmaster to find out what will work best. While it may be useful to work with others in his patrol on the same ranks, generally it is best for a new *older* boy to join a patrol of boys his same age. Catching up should be done with one-on-one work and by properly scheduling time and activities with clear goals on when to work on tasks and achieve merit badges and advancements. Merit badge colleges, clinics, and scout camps provide opportunities to complete many achievements in a short amount of time. Find out from your local district or council when local events are coming up.

Since around 18 months is the minimum amount of time to earn the Eagle rank (which must be completed by 18 years old), scouts starting at 16 years or older still should consider setting achievable goals — such as earning the First Class Rank and various merit badges.

Significant Requirements

The following is a list of significant efforts or long-term activities that the scout will need to accomplish toward his Eagle. Note that these are not the full requirements — be sure to check the real requirements in the up-to-date merit badge book, Boy Scout Handbook, or Boy Scout Requirements Handbook.

☐ Record the best results for some defined fitness exercises, practice for 30 days, and then record again to show improvement. (Tenderfoot rank)

☐ Camp 20 days and 20 nights at Scouting activities — some with hiking, backpacking, snowshoeing, skiing, biking, boating, rappelling, or snow camping. (Camping merit badge)

☐ 16 months of positions of responsibility. (Total for Star, Life, and Eagle ranks.)

☐ 13 hours of approved service. (Total for Second Class, Star, and Life ranks.)

☐ Volunteer eight hours at a charitable organization. (Citizenship in the Community merit badge)

☐ Obtain a physical examination using the official scout medical examination form. (Personal Fitness merit badge)

☐ Design and follow a 12-week physical fitness program. (Personal Fitness merit badge)

☐ Participate in an emergency service or practice drill with a community agency or the troop. (Emergency Preparedness merit badge) *

☐ Swim continuously for 400 yards. (Lifesaving merit badge)*

☐ Swim continuously for 150 yards. (Swimming merit badge)†

☐ Plan and hike five 10-mile hikes and a 20-mile hike on different days. (Hiking merit badge)†

☐ Cycle two 10-mile rides, two 15-mile rides, two 25-mile rides, and a 50-mile ride. (Cycling merit badge)†

---

*The scout only needs to earn one of the Lifesaving or Emergency Preparedness merit badges for the Eagle requirement.

†The scout only needs to earn one of the Swimming, Hiking, or Cycling merit badges for the Eagle requirement.

☐ Keep a journal while observing two small outdoor areas six different times. (Environmental Science merit badge)

☐ Track personal finances for 13 consecutive weeks. (Personal Management merit badge)

☐ Prepare and a follow a seven day schedule and keep a daily diary during this time. (Personal Management merit badge)

☐ Prepare a list of home chores and do them for 90 days keeping a record when each is done. (Family Life merit badge)

☐ Plan, lead, and document an approved Eagle project. (See chapter 13.)

In addition, the scout will need to write several reports of various lengths, prepare and lead presentations and give speeches, and meet and discuss with various experts about jobs and other skills.

In many cases, the boy should discuss the merit badge and rank requirements in advance with his counselors and leaders.

Keeping Track of Achievements

Accurately and easily being able to track requirements and being able to quickly share this information is important for boys, parents, leaders, and the troop as a whole. Knowing what upcoming tasks are still needed and organizing past results may be a stumbling block for some boy's advancements. Organization may help some boys advance quicker and keep them motivated.

The troop Advancement Chair (a position filled by an adult member of the troop committee) should keep an official record of each scout's advancement. This would include at minimum the ranks each scout has achieved and the merit badges he has earned. Additional items that the troop might track include service hours completed, nights of camping (to be applied toward the Camping merit badge), and rank requirements that have been signed off.

A software package can help a troop manage and automate advancement record keeping and other aspects of their unit. A few of the programs can monitor their data to notify about missing requirements or completed achievements. Some individuals or units may use generic database or spreadsheet software, such as Excel, to track troop or individual work. Scout-NET is BSA's official software-based record keeping system which allows the council to import and verify advancement records, rechartering, and enrollments electronically. The following lists a few troop management softwares:

BSAdv

> This is a component for the free Joomla content management system for managing unit data and advancement data for the troop. (It doesn't track an individual scout's advancement.) `http://sourceforge.net/projects/bsadv/`

ScoutingPlanner.com

> This commercial website service is used for meeting planning, advancement tracking, and communications between leaders, parents, and scouts. `http://scoutingplanner.com`

ScoutSoft

> This commercial software is ScoutNET certified and may be used to upload charters and advancement reports. It can generate Excel, JPEG, and PDF reports. It runs on Java-supported platforms. `http://www.scoutsoft.net/`

ScoutTrack.com

This website-based commercial software for parents, scouts, and leaders may be used to track advancements, merit badges, and service hours. It also provides a troop calendar and automated emails. `http://www.scouttrack.com/`

Trooper

This commercial software is designed for troops to track information for all troop members and the troop as a whole. It's not really geared towards individual record keeping. It is Windows-only and is not web-enabled. `http://www.srtware.com/trooper/`

TroopMaster

This commercial software is useful for individual scouts or parents. It is able to generate over 100 reports, such as campouts attended, merit badges earned, leadership rosters, tour permits, etc. It is Windows-only and not website-based (but it can synchronize data to an online database). TroopMaster is Scout-NET certified. (The company also provides financial ledger software for troops.) `http://www.troopmaster.com/products/boyscouts/boy_scouts.php`

TroopTrack

This commercial website service allows parents and scouts to review the scout's progress, check the troop calendar, and use email lists for the troop. `http://www.trooptrack.com/`

In addition, troops may also display large charts or boards which track individuals' advancements for the entire troop.

Even if the troop keeps good records, the most up-to-date copy of a scout's progress is usually in the back pages of his copy of the Boy Scout Handbook. This is where troop leaders have signed off his completed rank requirements. It's a good idea for

parents or guardians to photocopy the signed-off rank requirement pages every few months to verify the scout's progress in
the event that his handbook is lost or damaged. They can keep
these in the boy's scouting notebook or you may choose to use
separate file folders to track the scout progress. The boy's
personal records should be compared with the unit's records
periodically.

Maintaining a notebook of a scout's awards and achievements
will help him remember how far he has come in scouting. This
notebook can include completed blue cards, logs of service
hours and campouts, certificates of achievement, ribbons, and
special patches. The notebook can be started for a new scout
by a parent or guardian and maintained by the scout himself
as he gets older. It may be valuable at the boy's Eagle Board
of Review and items from the notebook can also be put on
display during his Eagle Court of Honor. At the end of his
scouting career, he'll have a priceless memento of the years he
spent as a Boy Scout.

Summary

- It is suggested that boys earn the First Class rank within
  their first year of scouting.

- Scouts should consider keeping a notebook, file folders,
  or a database to track their scouting goals, requirements
  progress, awards, and achievements.

- The troop calendar should include a variety of fun and
  challenging activities that appeal to all age groups.

11 Camping and Outdoor Activities

Outdoor activities and camping are key components of scouting. The early ranks require hiking; map, compass, and orienteering work; and identifying wild animals and plants. The early ranks also require pitching tents, overnight campouts, campout activities, and camp cooking. The Eagle rank requires the Camping merit badge which needs 20 nights of troop or patrol campouts (and only one week of summer or long-term camp may be used). Pioneering, Backpacking, Wilderness Survival, and many other merit badges provide outdoor possibilities.

Besides overnight campouts, scouts can experience the outdoors at resident summer camp, Camporees, and Jamborees. There are also High Adventure programs at the troop, council, and national level that allow scouts to experience more rugged camping in the wilderness. (These are covered in the following chapter.)

Many troops go camping every month, while troops that go camping only a few times a year could make it very difficult to finish early ranks or the Camping merit badge. Some troops have a requirement to schedule a minimum of ten nights per year (which may be a single week-long camp plus five other overnighters).

Boy Scouts of America recommends that each troop conduct at least four overnight campouts per year (and attend a BSA-approved long-term camp). Active troops that are located in areas with lots of camping opportunities might conduct eight to ten campouts per year. Commonly these are overnight on Fridays, Saturdays (ending on Sunday), or both. They may also be scheduled for other long weekends or days off from school. (LDS troops do not camp over Saturday nights nor on Sundays, except in rare cases.)

Some troops go "car camping" where they drive up with a huge amount of supplies — and other troops camp light-weight and hike into their overnight destinations. Troops may be fair weather campers and only go when it is not too hot and not too cold, while others are well prepared to camp in snow, rain, or extreme heat.

Troops may have a new-scout campout with a focus on preparation and basic camping skills for new scouts — and maybe even their parents.

Scout campouts often include an evening or campfire program. Sitting around a campfire, the troop may do yells, skits, songs, and listen to a Scoutmaster minute, motivational, and adventure stories. The event, usually an hour or less, may be somber or fun — or both. This is usually led by the Senior Patrol Leader who may arrange the participants ahead of time.

Planning Troop Outings

Many details must be considered when planning troop outings. Where to go and what to do may be decided by the PLC, but adults are needed to help with equipment, logistics, permits, and finances. Here is an overview of the items that need to be planned for each outing.

- Decide if the outing will have any specific focus or skills learning. Maybe invite experts or merit badge counselors to participate.

- Determine a date for the outing and put it on the troop calendar. If required, make campground reservations or obtain wilderness or backcountry permits.

- Determine the cost per scout for the outing, including travel, food, and camping fees.

- Communicate with scouts and parents about the outing. A flyer or web page that contains all necessary information is the best way to avoid confusion. The SPL should also announce the outing and create enthusiasm for it at troop meetings. Provide plenty of notice — at least several weeks in advance.

- Sign up scouts in advance to determine an exact head count. Obtain a signed permission slip from the parent or guardian of each scout who will be attending. Any important medical information should be included on the permission slip and discussed with adult leaders who will be attending.

- Once a headcount is known, find adult leaders and drivers. A minimum of two adult leaders, one of whom has complete BSA training, should attend. A good rule of thumb is one adult per patrol, which typically is about eight scouts. Maybe discourage too many adult leaders from attending.

- Obtain insurance coverage information from drivers. (Many troops keep this information on file.)

- Prepare and file a Council tour permit.

- The Scoutmaster and SPL should work with patrol leaders on meal and activity planning.

- An Assistant Scoutmaster or committee member in charge of equipment should work with the youth Quartermaster to make sure all equipment is ready to go.

- Parents should be provided with an emergency contact number.

- Before departure, make sure scouts have packed the right equipment and have their *Basic Essentials*. Remind them that the buddy system will be in effect during the outing.

Some of these tasks may be done by youth leaders and some by adult leaders or committee members. At least one adult who is attending each outing should have a copy of the BSA *Guide to Safe Scouting* and be familiar with the *Sweet 16 of BSA Safety*. The Guide to Safe Scouting (available in both print versions and online) is an important resource for troop leaders. It outlines the safety procedures scout leaders should follow during outdoor activities. These guidelines and policies help adult leaders avoid accidents and dangerous situations. They should also have the tour permit with them.

Camping Skills

The outdoor program is one of the main reasons that boys join BSA. Scouting promises adventure, learning, and responsibility. This promise is delivered through camping, hiking, backpacking, canoeing, swimming, and other outdoor experiences. The camping experience fosters independence and self-reliance while providing adventure. The outdoor program also helps scouts learn to appreciate the beauty of nature and respect the environment.

As part of a patrol, scouts learn to work as members of a team to meet outdoor challenges — finding a campsite, pitching their tents, preparing meals in the open, and following the principles of Leave No Trace. They become more independent and self-disciplined as they solve problems and use new skills (often new to urban boys and the indoor generation). These include:[1]

- Properly packing

---

[1] Adequately covering all these outdoor and camping skills would take another book. Consult the Boy Scout Handbook for camping tips.

- Choosing clothing and dressing properly
- Selecting a tent site
- Pitching a tent
- Preparing bed (and pad or mattress)
- Putting up and taking down camp structures
- Taking down a tent
- Putting away a sleeping bag
- Use of axe, hatchet, knife, and saw
- Gathering fire starting materials
- Starting a fire
- Completely putting out a fire
- Latrine setup (and usage)
- Using a camp stove
- Meal planning, preparation, and cooking
- Cleaning dishes
- Repacking while at campsite
- Camp cleanup
- Adjusting to weather
- Carrying gear
- Proactive safety
- Managing accidents and injuries

Scouts may learn these skills over a series of multiple campouts and other meetings and activities. Some boys may be frustrated as they realize the difficulties involved; while other boys are natural outdoorsmen and thoroughly enjoy the various tasks.

Camping is the arena where the values of scouting are put into practice. Because scouts have fun in the outdoors, they absorb knowledge and skills that couldn't be conveyed as well in troop meetings. The outdoor program keeps a troop alive and vibrant. Without a strong outdoor program, troop meetings can lose focus and fail to sustain boys' interest.

The outdoor program is also an attraction for adult volunteers. Helping scouts to plan and carry out a full and exciting outdoor program is one of the most satisfying parts of Boy Scout leadership.

Adult Supervision

The Scoutmaster and Assistant Scoutmasters are responsible for the troop's outdoor program and for supervising scouts on campouts. In order to carry out a successful program, the Scoutmaster and as many ASMs as possible should complete BSA Outdoor Leader Skills training. This training gives adults an overview of the same outdoor skills that scouts work on for the Tenderfoot, Second Class, and First Class ranks. It also conveys the importance of using the patrol method during campouts and teaches adults BSA safety procedures.

As long as one trained leader is present, a troop can decide which other adults go camping. If Assistant Scoutmasters aren't available, parents can be enlisted to provide adult supervision on campouts. Any adult who attends a campout should complete at minimum BSA Youth Protection Training, which covers some of the most basic safety practices including two-deep leadership, driving safety, and BSA policies on tobacco, alcohol, and drugs.

Boy Scout Outdoor Essentials

The Boy Scout Handbook provides a list of essential items that each scout should have for most outdoor activities. These are called The Scout Basic Essentials (also referred to as the Ten Essentials).

The first ten items on the list below are the Scout Basic Essentials. It also includes several additional items that are often found to be very useful on hikes and campouts. A few of these items could be critical to a scout's survival if he were lost in a wilderness area. The scout should know what each item is used for and how to use it.

All of the essentials with the exception of extra clothing can be stored in a large Ziploc bag which is then placed in a day pack or backpack. A transparent Ziploc bag makes it easier for the scout to see exactly what is in the bag. The essentials can be stored in the bag between outings so they'll always be handy and won't need to be assembled each time they're needed.

- ☐ Pocketknife — Should have a sharp blade (stainless steel is best). Avoid knives with too many blades and gadgets.

- ☐ First Aid Kit — Should include band aids, tape, gauze pads, moleskin for blisters, insect repellant, disinfectant, and lip balm.

- ☐ Extra Clothing — Be prepared for changes in the weather with extra clothing that can be layered.

- ☐ Rain Gear — Include a waterproof poncho or lightweight parka that can be folded into a small bag.

- ☐ Water Bottle — At least a one-quart bottle filled with water. Respect the principles of Leave No Trace by using a non-disposable bottle.

- ☐ Flashlight — A smaller LED flashlight that uses AA or AAA batteries is easiest to carry. Some scouts prefer an

LED headlamp that keeps their hands free for camping tasks.

☐ Trail Food — High-energy snack food should be packed for an emergency.

☐ Matches and Fire Starters — Strike-anywhere, waterproof matches or a butane lighter should be stored in a waterproof container.

☐ Sun Protection — SPF 15 or greater sunscreen is a necessity; a wide-brimmed hat and sunglasses may also be included.

☐ Map and Compass — The compass should be liquid filled and have a housing with a straight edge. The map should be specific to the current outing. A scout might want to take along a GPS device for fun, but it should not be a substitute for map and compass and knowing how to use them.

Other Essentials

☐ Extra Batteries — Place extra batteries for the flashlight in a small plastic bag.

☐ Plastic Garbage Bags — 2 or 3 heavy-weight garbage bags can be used for a variety of purposes including rain poncho, shelter, and ground cover.

☐ Mylar Emergency Blanket — Retains body heat in case of emergency.

☐ Mirror or Signaling Device — The scout should know how to use the device to signal for help in case of emergency.

☐ Rope — 50 feet of braided nylon rope is useful for a variety of purposes.

☐ Whistle — The scout should be instructed to only use the whistle in an emergency (such as signaling where he is when lost)

☐ Toilet Paper and Trowel — An essential item for backcountry outings, this may even come in handy when a campground restroom is out of toilet paper. An entire roll isn't needed; just place a few sheets in a small plastic bag. Also include an extra plastic bag for disposal of used paper.

☐ Note pad and pen or pencil — For writing down directions or taking notes about things seen along the trail.

Food

Ideally, patrols plan and cook meals together as a group. The menu is either created by the patrol together or by a scout who is working on some requirement where meal planning is required. Each patrol member may have a duty related to the meal (e.g. fire preparation, food preparation, cleanup, etc.), possibly with the assignments rotated between meals.

The patrol members may be assigned responsibility for providing a portion of the meal. Many troops just have families purchase their own food for the boy and don't use the troop's budget. In some troops, the adult leaders shop for food and supplies. A normal amount of money is around $10 per boy for an overnight campout with a few meals and snacks. Turn in receipts as soon as possible to get reimbursed (if purchasing for a group). Another option is a buddy system for sharing food costs; for example, one boy may provide dinner and the other boy provides breakfast for two. Troops may have food supplies or even a troop refrigerator.

Talk to your patrol leader or patrol cook (or Grubmaster) to learn the procedures for meals at campouts.

Camping Gear

The scout should ask his patrol leader about what gear is required. Some troops or patrols provide camping gear checklists.

The Quartermaster is the boy who keeps track of the troop's gear. Many troops own tents, camp stoves, and other camping equipment. Boys may choose to use the troop's gear or their own and share as needed. Find out from your troop what they can provide or to learn what you need.

You should also know what is not allowed to bring. Commonly boom boxes, handheld video games, radios, mini TV's, MP3 players, cell phones, and other electronic devices (with the possible exception of cameras and GPS devices) aren't permitted.

Your troop may have a trip binder or folder that contains planners for camping and menus, shopping lists, duty rosters, tour permits, drivers, phone lists, and more.

When backpacking or carrying in supplies, be extra prepared and attentive to over-packing, too large of a pack, comfortable shoes, etc.

Individual Camp Gear List

In addition to the essential items listed earlier, common camping gear for a single scout include:

- ☐ Clothing (per season and weather)
- ☐ Backpack
- ☐ Sleeping bag
- ☐ Sleeping pad
- ☐ Ground cloth
- ☐ Plate

- ☐ Spoon
- ☐ Bowl
- ☐ Cup
- ☐ Soap
- ☐ Toothbrush and toothpaste
- ☐ Comb
- ☐ Small towel

Optional Camp Gear List

- ☐ Dental floss
- ☐ Watch
- ☐ Fork
- ☐ Camera
- ☐ Swimsuit
- ☐ Fishing pole and gear

Group Camp Gear List

Beyond an individual scout, the patrol or troop needs may include:

- ☐ Tent, ground cloths, tarps, stakes
- ☐ Dining fly, cords, and stakes
- ☐ Stove(s) and fuel
- ☐ Garbage bags
- ☐ Spade or small shovel
- ☐ Pots and pans (per menu)

☐ Tongs or hot pads (as needed)

☐ Plastic sheets for food preparation surface

☐ Utensils, such as large spoon or spatula (per menu)

☐ Soap

☐ Cleaning pad or cloth

☐ Repair kit (thread, needles, safety pins)

☐ Large water container

☐ Water filter or tablets

☐ Long cords or ropes

☐ U.S.A. flag and Patrol flag

Summary

- The Eagle Scout rank (via the Camping merit badge) requires 20 nights of scout campouts.

- Troops normally have four or five overnighters a year plus a week of summer camp.

- Scouts learn outdoor skills and personal responsibility by preparing for and attending campouts.

12 Summer Camps, High Adventure, and Special Events

Boy Scouting provides many opportunities for long-term resident camping, advanced outdoor adventures, and various special events, such as Scouting Jamborees and district camporees.

Summer Camp

The troop attends the summer camp together as a group. The troop has their own campsite, dining tables, and meets together for ceremonies and other camp-wide meetings.

Summer camps are usually six to seven days long and commonly begin on Sunday and end on Saturday. (LDS troops often arrive early on Monday.) Generally it is well organized by the local council. Some vicinities may have multiple camp possibilities — different locations and/or many dates to choose from. Many units plan and design their own week-long camping event — this will be introduced later in the "high adventure" topic. Some units attend camps hours from their home or in a different state. Camps often host five to 15 troops of all different sizes (from 5 boys to 50 boys for example).

Summer camps are staffed by paid and volunteer adult and youth leaders including a nurse or medical professional. The head leader is called the Camp Director. In some cases, the camp staff — who help lead activities and teach crafts and merit badges — may be younger than the camp attendees. Some camps assign a youth staff member to be a liaison for the troop during the week — they are available for questions and often may participate with some of your troop's weekly activities.

Camps cost between $100 to $350 per week per boy. In some cases, a couple of adult leaders for the troop are included for free. The pricing depends on the location and on what the camp provides. Usually summer camps have a camp store that sells t-shirts, hats, pocket knives, snacks, drinks, supplies for merit badge requirements or crafts, bug spray, camp supplies, etc. Some parents have their children earn their own money for camp extras and other parents supply their child with an abundance of money. Sometimes, Scoutmasters may hold and keep track of money for younger scouts as needed.

Often troops need to register and pay for their week of camp several months prior to the event.

Scouts and leaders usually need to have a medical physical examination[1] using an official BSA form signed by their own doctor submitted for the camp. The camp's medical director will keep it on file and the Scoutmaster may also have a copy. This usually needs to be renewed yearly. (So if your following year's week of camp is before the physical expires you may be able to use it again.)

Most camps have swimming in a lake or pool (or both) and may have watercraft activities, like rowboating, canoeing, kayaking, and even sailboarding and sailing at some camps. Swim tests are required. In some cases, troops do their swim tests prior to attending camp and others do it at camp on the first day. The scouts are classified as a swimmer, beginner, or as

---

[1] A physical examination is needed for activities that are three days or longer.

a non-swimmer (or non-participants). The beginner test involves jumping into water over the swimmer's head, swimming 25 feet, coming to a stop, turning around, and then swimming back to starting point. The swimmer test (also a requirement for the First Class Rank) includes jumping into water over the swimmer's head, continuously and strongly swimming 75 yards (using breast, crawl, side, or trudgen strokes) with at least one sharp turn, then 25 yards using an easy backstroke, and completed with a resting float. Generally these tests are supervised by a certified lifeguard or aquatics instructor.

The swim and boating areas commonly require a buddy system. Many camps keep tokens or cards on a board that represent the swimmers. Periodically the lifeguards may call for a buddy check or roll call of the swimmers.

Commonly, troops will be able to sign up for their own camp site which may include an outhouse, running water, camp fire area, picnic table(s), and a covered area. They may also provide A-frame canvas tent-cabins on wooden platforms and cots. (Some camps may charge extra for cots.) The campsite may be distant from others troops, such as separated by trees and creeks, and may even be a long walk (like ten minutes or a quarter mile) from the main lodge or meeting area. Other camps may have all the units camped in the same field, tightly packed with many tents. Troops often decorate their campsites with flags, wooden pole fences, signs, or other ways to identify their troop or patrols. Depending on the camp setup and troop needs, the campsite may be separated for each patrol. In some cases, small troops may share large campsites.

Individual or group showers are often provided. Note that some boys go the entire week without showering — so at least encourage them to go swimming and take a shower after that.

Many camps provide meals prepared by a paid cooking staff and eaten in a lodge or cafeteria. Other camps may provide food which is prepared and eaten at the troop's own campsite. (Some troops alternate this yearly.) Troops usually need to provide volunteers for the kitchen, dishwashers, or cafeteria setup and/or cleanup. Some troops provide their own kitchen storage cupboard, washbasins, and tables. (Troops may even own their own trailers for hauling equipment for summer camp.) Patrols may have their own Patrol Cook — a youth leader in charge of supervising the kitchen and delegating cooking and cleanup work. Everyone helps.

Camp activities may include religious services, singing in the lodge, campfire stories, day hikes, swimming, canoeing, and daily flag ceremonies with troop roll calls. Troops may be assigned or given the opportunity to lead some of the camp-wide activities. Some troops or patrols carry their unique flags and have their own cheers. Depending on your troop or camp policies, the boys may stay together as patrols or use a buddy system.

The week long scout camp is a great opportunity for the boys to work on many requirements for ranks and a diverse range of merit badges. Usually official scout camps will have counselors for around 10 to 20 (or more) different merit badges. It is encouraged for the boys to sign up for the scheduled classes and some boys may be able to complete at least a few merit badges during the week. Ambitious boys may earn six or seven or more merit badges in the week, but it is common to usually sign up for a few merit badges. Four or five merit badges may be a good amount for a young scout so they can also enjoy the other camp opportunities. Many consider it easier and faster to earn merit badges in the week-long camp setting. Scoutmasters usually have the opportunity to sign up the scouts for their preferred merit badges weeks and even months before the week of camp. The scout may want to plan ahead for the merit badges taken at camp by reading the pamphlets and discussing requirements with others. Maybe some requirements can be done before camp too. The scouts should not over schedule and may want to sign up for a mix of fun and also challenging merit badges.

The classes and activities may be spread out over the week at specific times. It is a good idea to have someone with a watch to help keep track of time. Also in some units, the Scoutmaster also keeps an itinerary for all his boys' classes and activities.

A scout that attends summer camp in his first year is far more likely to be in scouts 12 months later than one who didn't. For many troops, camp is only attended by the younger scouts, such as those in their first three years.[2] (The older boys move to other, more adventuresome activities.) Often camps also have a dedicated First Class course of study for younger or new boys with a focus on accomplishing the requirements for the Tenderfoot, Second Class, and First Class ranks.

In addition to registered classes, camps often have unregistered, drop-in activities — such as swimming, canoeing, basket weaving, carving, pioneering (building with ropes and poles), and day hikes — for fun or even to work on achievements. Camps also have patrol or troop competitions, such as triathlons, boat races, and dodgeball. A fun activity common at camp is the canoe swamp — for the Canoeing merit badge, the boy must capsize a canoe; there may also be contests or battles where the boys *swamp* other's canoes.

Two concerns or problems with scout camp include: homesickness and lack of discipline.

Week-long summer camp is often a child's first long-term independence from their own family. Homesickness is defined as melancholy or being distressed from being away from home or family. Research shows that at least 80% of all boys have some level of homesickness but less than ten percent is severe. Tips for preparing for camp include encouraging your child's independence and practice separations throughout the year (such as normal scout overnight campouts), discussing what camp will be like before he goes to camp, role playing, packing a

---

[2]Note that LDS troops do not send 11-year-old scouts to week-long camps.

personal or fun item from home (but make sure it is okay for your troop and camp's policies), and sending a letter or care package ahead of time to arrive the first day or during the week of camp. Also find out your troop's and camp's phone availability or phone call policies. (It is also commonly suggested to not bribe boys nor suggest offering early pickup.) Camp is a great opportunity to learn independence and confidence.

Lack of discipline covers: boisterous, unsupervised boys causing perceived trouble — or quiet and tired boys who don't attend classes or join activities. The keys for helping solve this are the same for having a successful camp:

- It is important that the boys signup for and attend classes that interest them and also they are capable of learning and accomplishing.

- Have a camp calendar or schedule that shows the camp-wide activities, eating and meeting times, and individual class schedules.

- Have a camp map so the boys (and leaders) can find where to go.

Also be sure that the boys know to drink lots of water and eat adequately and get enough rest during the week. Camps have defined bed time, quiet time, or lights out — plus an early wakeup and early flag ceremony.

Special Events

Several traditional BSA special events give scouts the opportunity to interact with scouts and Scouters from other troops.

Scout-O-Rama

This is a Scouting festival that involves both Cub Scouts and Boy Scouts from a district or council.

The public is invited to attend to see the Scouting program in action. Troops and packs set up booths that feature demonstrations, games, and cooking. At some Scout-O-Ramas, scouts can earn merit badges and participate in adventures like climbing rock walls.

Camporee

This is an annual district or council event where troops compete as patrols in competitions that include scout skills like first aid, knot tying, fire building, emergency preparedness, orienteering (compass), pioneering (lashing), and cooking. A camporee typically takes place over a weekend campout and may be planned around a theme. There is usually a campfire with skits and songs and an awards ceremony on the final day.

National Jamboree

BSA holds a National Jamboree once every 4 years (with the exception of 2010, which was held after 5 years to coincide with the 100th anniversary of Boy Scouts of America). Referred to by many attendees as *Jambo*, this event is an experience a scout will never forget. Scouts who attend are placed into special Jambo troops at the council level and up to 18 months of preparation takes place. During Jamboree, scouts have the opportunity to participate in activities, watch demonstrations and trade patches. Recent Jamborees have been held at Fort A.P. Hill in Virginia and attended by more than 40,000 scouts and leaders and visited by 300,000 members of the public. In 2013, National Jamboree will be held at the new Summit Bechtel Family National Scout Reserve in West Virginia and will include High Adventure activities.

World Jamboree

The World Organization of the Scout Movement (WOSM) hosts a World Jamboree every four years in different locations throughout the world. About 30,000 — 40,000 scouts (both boys and girls) and leaders have attended recent World Jamborees in Thailand, the United Kingdom, and Sweden. In 2019, World Jamboree will be held at the Summit Bechtel Family National Scout Reserve in West Virginia.

High Adventure

BSA keeps older youth interested through High Adventure outdoor activities. Scouts aged 13 and older can participate in long-distance wilderness backpacking, rock climbing, rafting, scuba diving, sailing, caving, and a variety of other exciting outdoor activities. High adventures require physical and mental preparation and are often difficult — but rewarding — events.

A troop that has leaders who are experienced in High Adventure activities can plan their own outings, such as backpacking for a week along the Appalachian Trail, canoeing for a few days in the Cascade Mountains, or deep-sea fishing in the Gulf of Mexico. A common example is the *Fifty Miler* — a backpacking or canoeing trip which often is a highlight of the boy's scouting years. (See page 80 about the 50-Miler Award.)

If adults are interested in High Adventure but lack experience, many councils offer High Adventure training. Besides troop-sponsored High Adventure outings, local councils across the U.S. offer High Adventure programs that are open to any troop. More information about these programs can be found on Scouting.org:

http://www.scouting.org/scoutsource/BoyScouts/Resources/
olderboyadventure.aspx

Scouts and leaders can also participate in High Adventure programs at these national High Adventure bases:

Philmont Scout Ranch

Located in New Mexico and covering more than 214 square miles, this is BSA's largest High Adventure camp. Scouts and leaders in crews of 7 to 12 complete backpacking expeditions that include trail camps and organized programs in staffed camps.

Florida Sea Base

A variety of boating, fishing, snorkeling, and scuba-diving programs are offered at this High Adventure Base in the Florida Keys and an affiliated Sea Base in the Bahamas.

Northern Tier Bases

This collection of High Adventure bases in Minnesota and Canada offers wilderness canoe trips that cover 50 to 150 miles. The Charles L. Sommers Canoe Base in Minnesota also offers a cold weather camping program that includes cross-country skiing, dog sledding, ice fishing, and other winter activities.

The high adventure is usually hard work — physically and mentally — such as hiking or canoeing many miles, day after day. Troops should prepare by building up related strength, stamina, and knowledge on earlier activities.

Costs

Camps, jamborees, high adventures, and other activities may have significant costs. Generally troops will not require a lot of out-of-pocket, but plan money earning projects to earn funds for the entire unit. Nevertheless, some troops may require payment schedules to help pay for participation. (Paying for events is discussed starting on page 43.)

Summary

- Week-long summer camps provide scouts with fun activities and many opportunities for various requirements progress.

- Special events such as Scout-O-Rama festivals, area camporees, and National and World Jamborees provide scouts opportunities to meet many other scouts.

- High adventures provide experienced scouts with physically and mentally challenging — and fun —- activities, such as multi-day and many-mile backpacking and canoeing trips, rock climbing, sailing, and deep-sea fishing trips.

13 Earning the Eagle

The Eagle Scout Rank is often seen as the final visible, tangible goal of scouting. The earlier ranks are stepping stones in both experiences and actual requirements to earning the Eagle. It basically requires the same standard requirements as the other ranks, but also includes various paperwork and the Eagle project which is a boy-planned and boy-led service project of substantial benefit.

These final steps may be complex, but hopefully this chapter can lead you through this maze. This chapter discusses the key Eagle requirements, the Eagle project and paperwork, completing the Eagle application, the Eagle Board of Review, the special Court of Honor, and continuing after the Eagle is awarded.

The scout does not need to wait until the merit badges requirement is completed to begin planning his Eagle project. (See chapter 8 for details on the merit badge requirements.) The project planning may begin as soon as the scout passes his Life rank Board of Review. (Make sure that date is recorded.) But the actual project work cannot begin until it is approved multiple times.

Age

The youngest possible age to earn the Eagle rank is mostly undefined. A boy may start Boy Scouting if 10 years old and has completed the fifth grade or earned the Arrow of Light in

Cub Scouts. There are no rank requirements based on ages. The first three Boy Scout ranks do not have a time requirement, but they do require at least ten separate activities — including three campouts — other than normal troop or patrol meetings. The final three ranks have a total time requirement of 16 months and the Eagle rank needs (via the Camping merit badge) 17 additional nights of camping. Commonly, a boy begins at age 11, and if the troop (or patrol) provides one campout or other additional activity every month, potentially a boy could complete his Eagle in 26 months. In a minimum situation, a scout could earn his Eagle in over 16 months to 20 months. Ideally, the boy will have earned his First Class within the first year and at least one rank per year afterward.

Some Scoutmasters say that boys should not earn their Eagle before a certain age, such as 14, 15, or even 16 years old — and may even discourage quick young advancement. (But they should not create their own criteria to hold boys back.) The opposite argument is that boys may lose interest or needed time after 15 or 16 years old — and some Scoutmasters believe 14 is a good age when to complete the Eagle. It is likely that a boy completing requirements at 16 or 17 years old may have significantly different learning experiences than a 12 or 13 year old. Some say that older boys gain and understand more, while younger boys may have had their work wrongly done by zealous parents or leaders.

The project and all Eagle requirements must be completed before the boy turns 18, except the Board of Review may be shortly after.

Official Application and Paperwork

The Eagle Scout Rank requires official forms to be completed, signed (by multiple people), and submitted. At the time of this book printing, the official Eagle Scout Rank Application is BSA Publication #512-728 (2010 printing).

Note that the application's requirements differ slightly than the Boy Scout Handbook and Boy Scout Requirements book. Follow the application. In some cases, it is slight wording or clarifications.

The application asks for an attachment that contains a statement from the boy about his ambitions and life purpose and a listing of positions the boy held that show his leadership skills in the community or at camp, school, church, or for other organizations. This may answer what he plans for the upcoming stages of his life and what he does outside of scouting. If he received any awards, certificates, honors, or other recognitions related to his service, he should mention them also.

At the time of this book printing, The Eagle Scout Leadership Service Project Workbook is BSA Publication #512-927 (2009 printing). This is the project plan and using it is required. It should be neat and preferably typed. Some scouts type and print to separate sheets of paper and cut and paste or attach to the workbook as needed. Completing this long workbook is covered in the upcoming sections.

The scout should ask for the application and workbook from his troop committee, Scoutmaster, or Eagle Advisor (upcoming section), or obtain them from the local district or council office. Or he may print out a PDF as downloaded from the Internet. The official download website for the scout forms is at

`http://www.scouting.org/scoutsource/media/forms.aspx`

The writing (or typing) in the application, workbook, and for the individual statement should be neat, well organized, and written in complete understandable sentences. The scout should use correct spelling and proper grammar. He may need to update or retype as needed. He may ask for others to review the application or to provide assistance as needed.

The Eagle Advisor

Often troops have a committee member or assistant Scoutmaster who has the role of being the Eagle coordinator, counselor, or advisor. This adult is responsible for working with boys to guide them through preparing and submitting their Eagle Scout application and workbook. They may also assist with brainstorming on project ideas and planning. If you or the boy has any questions about his Eagle steps, ask the Eagle advisor. The Eagle advisor may coach and encourage the boy on his progress.

In addition, the district has responsibility for advisement, and almost every district has members of the advancement committee ready to assist an Eagle candidate with project development, paperwork, etc.

Character References

The Eagle rank requires character references. The boy needs to supply multiple names of those who will provide a recommendation. These should be people the boy personally knows. These may be parents, religious leaders, coaches, teachers, school guidance counselors, and employers for example. The application has room for six references with address, telephone, and email. (It is understood that some scouts do not have a religious affiliation or may not have had an employer.) The scout should ask the references first before providing their details.

Ask your unit or council if they have an Eagle Scout Reference Form that they would like the scout to use. Some have the scouts provide a form and a pre-addressed stamped envelope to gather a confidential response. This response is sent to the council or district and not to the scout.

This is generally a casual or formal letter recommending the boy as an Eagle Scout. It may address his integrity and character traits that make him suitable as an Eagle. It may share examples as known by the adult illustrating the boy's qualifications.

Eagle Scout Leadership Service Project

The Eagle project is planned, developed, organized, and led by the boy. Leading the project from start to finish is often a highlight of the boy's life. It allows the scout to use and further develop his scouting leadership skills and knowledge to benefit others.

Keep a Log

The boy should keep a log or calendar of all the days and amount of time spent on planning, researching, and leading their project. This includes discussions with scoutmasters, Eagle coordinators, and other advisors, phone calls, and other communications. The scout may want to write complete and detailed sentences so they can be easily understood or re-used later for the final report. Extra notes may be useful also as reminders.

It is highly advisable that the boy takes pictures, gets things in writing, and saves every document he can possibly muster for his project. He should compile them in orderly fashion for the board to look over. The more thorough his notes — the more valuable it is to the Board of Review.

Choose a Project

The Eagle project needs to involve imagination, planning, and supervision. Regular, ongoing service is not considered. The project may not begin before the Life rank is accomplished — this is expected since the project must be approved ahead of time. The project must be completed before the Eagle Board of Review.

The project may not be done for any profit-making organization or business. The project also cannot benefit the Boy Scouts of America directly, including your troop or council property. The project may not be planned and led by multiple scouts — only one scout may use a single Eagle project.[1]

Blood drives and other donation drives are often not considered worthy as an Eagle project. Some involve little creativity and recipient organizations often have the procedure fine-tuned leaving little need of planning or leading by the scout. If the scout desires to plan and lead a collection drive, he should be careful to define very high expectations and a clear plan of how this will be different from routine drives.

The scout should make sure he follows the troop's, district's, and council's recommendations or requirements related to choosing a Eagle project. They may have some wishes or demands that will make the project easier to be accepted.

The project should be *helpful* for your community, a school, or a religious institution.

The scout may want to brainstorm ideas and write a long list. He may ask others, visit websites, and discuss with his Eagle advisor and Scoutmaster to find more ideas or to fine-tune his list. Questions he may want to discuss are:

- Who will benefit from the project?

- How will it be accomplished?

- Will I be proud of this project?

---

[1] Of course, other scouts may assist to earn service time for earlier ranks as approved by their Scoutmaster or corresponding merit badge counselor.

- Will I be able to demonstrate leadership?

As the scout narrows down his list, he may meet or talk with representatives of the organizations who would benefit from the service project. (From his many experiences with contacting merit badge counselors, it should be easy for the scout to find and contact the group and a specific representative there.)

The boy should log this time in researching ideas and who he discussed potential projects with.

After the scout has discussed his chosen plan with his Scoutmaster and group representative, he should start writing his initial project plan in the official workbook.

Some troops require the boy to make a proposal in front of the local troop committee, but it is not part of the standard requirements, application, or workbook. Ask your Scoutmaster about this to find out if the committee wants to have a brief proposal which may be done before the lengthy initial write-up or if the committee as a group prefers to see the final plan. (Note that a committee member signs the final plan to approve it; this is discussed in a following section.)

Initial Project Plan

The workbook provides a few pages for the boy to complete to describe his project and planning. The sections include:

- Project name
- Project description
- The group it benefits
- Why it benefits this group
- Date when discussed with unit leader
- Signature from the group's representative
- Present situation and planning details

- Drawings / illustrated plans

- Before photos

The initial project description is a half-page brief explanation without specific planning steps. It is a short summary used to quickly and simply introduce the organization and defines the service to be provided. It next lists the name and contact information for the group and the scout writes a half page why the project will benefit this group and what community may enjoy its results. The date the concept was discussed with a Scoutmaster (unit leader) or Eagle advisor is documented.

The representative from the community, church or religious institution, or school who will benefit from the service also signs the workbook saying they discussed the idea or concept with the scout. Note that a representative of the group receiving the service signs the workbook *three* times: 1) discussed the project; 2) approved the project plan; and 3) when the project is completed.

The project details section is a few pages long. This is the detailed plan that describes the current condition or situation and how the project will be directed. This section does not need to restate the benefits. The scout should clearly list and explain how to carry out the project step-by-step. He may want to consider writing it as thoroughly as if he was not around to lead the project — so it should answer any questions or help solve problems volunteers may get.

Topics to be covered and questions to be answered by the scout in this detailed plan may include:

- Where will the work be done? Will the materials of near-completed project be moved? How?

- What to do about weather changes? (Such as raining when needing to paint outdoors.)

- How will volunteers get to the destinations? Who will transport supplies, tools, and materials? Any special types of transportation needed, like a truck bed or a vehicle towing a trailer. Who will drive?

- How will the event be announced? How will volunteers be found? Will posters, invitations, or flyers be distributed to get help (volunteers and/or supplies)? Any letters and other written or printed information?

- What materials are needed?

- What supplies need to be purchased? This may include a shopping list with specifications, sizes, item count, costs, etc. It may need to be specific with quality, finish, brand, item, and model numbers.

- What will be donated? How will these donations be procured?

- What tools are needed? What types? How many? Who will use? Any adult or experience restrictions for certain tools? What can be reused, borrowed, or bought? What is done with purchased tools after the project?

- What expendable supplies, like garbage bags, markers, drop cloths, disposable paint trays, fuel, posters, and other things? Where will you get these? What will you do with them when completed?

- What will be borrowed? How will you keep track?

- Who will take photos? What camera? Developing?

- What about drinks, water, and refreshments?

- What other costs or possible fees?

- Who will pay for needed supplies? How to get monetary donations?

- How to evaluate or judge completion?

- Who will do the work? (Do not need to name anyone specifically.) What organizations are they from? How and where will you find volunteers? Do you need any special skills or experts? How will you recruit them?

- Will the volunteers be grouped into certain times or days, or specific tasks?

- Will the volunteers need to be taught skills ahead of time or during the event?

- Who are the adult supervisors? Will anyone be needed for double-checking work or providing expertise? (Scout activities should be supervised by two adults, one with Youth Protection certification. See page 31 for details. Of course, the adults will not lead the Eagle project.)

- How will you make the project safe? Do you have any safety guidelines?

- What is needed for cleanup? Who will do cleanup? Any cleanup supplies needed?

Many Eagle projects have monetary costs. The project may involve fund-raising to finance project needs. The group benefiting from the project may have funds to assist with paying for supplies, but do not assume this. Funds should not be used to pay for labor. It is imperative that a boy keep a detailed ledger if he has raised funds to pay for materials. He must return unused funds to the donors.

This write up should also include step-by-step directions for the volunteers to follow. These instructions explain every task in order, including setup and cleanup.

In addition, the plan should include a schedule, timeline, or calendar that lists when the tasks will be started and completed.

The scout may want to discuss the planning steps before writing them up with his Eagle advisor, Scoutmaster, or experts related to his service work to help clearly explain the needs and schedule the time.

Note that this detailed project plan is used to direct and complete the project — and also to discuss the project work and success during the Board of Review.

The details may also need to describe the work environment and surroundings to help explain the work. Drawings and illustrations may be useful to further illustrate the steps, design, and project as needed. (Use graph paper if applicable.) Photos or pictures of other completed, similar projects may be useful. On location photos taken before the project are also good.

Approvals

The detailed project plan must be approved by four people:

- Group representative

- Scoutmaster

- Unit committee member

- District or council advancement committee member

The scout should show his detailed plan to the group benefiting from the planned service. This representative approves it with a signature. The Scoutmaster also reviews and signs the plan.

The project plan also needs to be approved and signed by a troop committee member. As mentioned previously, the scout may need to present his project plan to the troop committee as a group (even though this requirement is neither clear nor consistent). The scout (or Scoutmaster) may contact the committee to schedule for the boy to present his project plan proposal. Wearing a Field Uniform, the boy introduces himself and shares his printed plan and discusses it. Generally this would just be a brief two to three minutes, but may be longer if the committee has many questions. A member of the committee, such as the Troop Committee Chairman, then approves the plan with a signature.

Next the scout needs to schedule to present the project plan to his district or council's advancement committee. Ask the Scoutmaster or troop committee to help know who to contact about this. The scout shows up on time wearing his full Field Uniform to present to the District (or Council) Advancement Committee for approval. They sign the workbook also. (In some cases, long distance may require a phone or email approval.)

The scout may want to make photocopies of the entire workbook just in case one is lost.

Project Management (Conducting the Project)

The scout cannot begin actually working on the project until he has received the four approval signatures, including the district's (or council's) advancement committee's okay.

Leading up to the day(s) of the event, the scout may continue to fine-tune and communicate his plan. He will recruit volunteers and assign specific tasks with clear and maybe written instructions. On the days of the event, the scout will coordinate, supervise, monitor and evaluate, guide, share examples, delegate, problem solve, and express praise, encouragement, and gratitude. He will lead.

If a boy must modify his project while it is in progress, he should secure the reasons in writing and approvals required. This is imperative when it substantially changes the scope or nature of the project. If a boy is approved to do one thing, and does it differently, he needs to have at minimum the approval of the receiving organization, but should also get the same person who approved the project to allow it to continue. If it isn't going to pass the Board of Review, he needs to know now — not after his modified project is completed.

At the end of the project, the previously-planned and scheduled clean-up procedures are followed and supplies and tools returned.

The scout should continue to keep a log of his and other's efforts on the project. A sign in / sign out time sheet may be used to list who assisted and how much time was volunteered. The boy and/or his volunteers may take photos to help document the work in progress and its completion.

After the event, the scout can send thank you notes as appropriate.

Final Report

The final section in the workbook is the write-up about carrying out the project. Often this is the greatest delay to submitting the Eagle paperwork. While the planning and event is in progress, the scout should consider writing in his log or calendar daily. Then he should complete his workbook as soon as possible before forgetting details. A good idea is to set a goal and plan to have the write-up completed within ten days (for example) after the project.

This includes documenting the hours the scout spent planning and leading the project. It also lists volunteers by name and their time worked. (Note that there is no minimum time requirement.) The scout also documents the materials used (or supplies bought) and their costs, donations received, and tools borrowed.

In addition, the scout briefly describes how and why he strayed from the initial plan and show approval(s) for the changes as applicable. The scout can compare his initial plan and his updated plans and then write how his checklists, dates, needs, supplies, finances, volunteer personnel, and other things had changed. He may explain if these changes were good or bad, helpful or disruptive.

Photos may also be copy and pasted or attached as extra sheets and clearly labeled to show the different steps of the project and the project's final results.

The scout also signs his report in the workbook. The scout may consider having his advisor review his final report before submitting it to his Scoutmaster and group representative who sign it again after the project is completed.

Scoutmaster Conference

After completing the project and all the other requirements (such as merit badges, six month Life time, and six month position of responsibility), the scout needs to have his conference with the Scoutmaster. (The Scoutmaster Conference is introduced on page 63.) This conference for the Eagle candidate may be in more detail and may be a good time to again go over all the details on the Eagle Scout Rank Application and the Eagle Scout Leadership Service Project Workbook.

In addition, the Scoutmaster may go over the boy's written (or typed) statement about his ambitions, life purpose, and leadership positions beyond just scouting.

Complete the Application and Submit the Paperwork

The Eagle application should be completed. It lists the dates when the boy became a Boy Scout (and Varsity Scout and Venturer if applicable), and passed his First Class Board of Review, Star Scout Board of Review, and Life Scout Board of Review. In addition, the scout lists the dates when the required and additional merit badges were earned and when positions of responsibility were held (while a Life Scout).

After getting the signatures from the Scoutmaster and committee chairman (indicating their approval and recommendation) on the application and the signatures from the Scoutmaster (again) and the representative of the group served by the Eagle project at the end of the workbook, these documents and the statement about himself should be promptly submitted to your local council service center. You may want to make photocopies as needed (such as new signed pages) before submitting.

The references listed on the application will be contacted.[2] The contents of the application will be certified as accurate and it will be confirmed that the scout is a registered member of his unit.

In some cases, the paperwork may be returned due to bad appearance, spelling issues, messy, in pencil, incomplete, inaccurate, or simply not neat.

The Eagle Board of Review

After the references verification and application certification, the boy will be contacted by an Eagle Scout Board of Review chairman to set the Board of Review date. Local councils or districts hold an official Eagle Board of Review. (The earlier Board of Reviews are covered on page 64.) In some cases, you may need to contact the local district (or council) to find out who to contact or how to setup and prepare for the appointment. They will require the Eagle application and project paperwork in advance.

The board will consist of three to six adults. The boy's guardians, relatives, or leaders will not serve on the board. Note that the Eagle board members probably do not know the scout.

---

[2]The council will not delay a Board of Review if the board doesn't receive the references' letters.

In some cases, the Eagle board of review is conducted at the unit level — in this case, a district or council advancement representative must be a member of the Eagle board.

Generally the scout will meet in a conference room at the council offices (or service center) in full Field Uniform (of course). His Scoutmaster (unless he is a parent or relative) usually joins and introduces the scout. The Scoutmaster doesn't participate on the board if he remains in the room. No relative or guardian may attend the Board of Review.

There are no defined questions that may be asked. The scout should respond clearly and act confidently. His years of Board of Review and other scouting experiences would have provided him with the speaking experience for this.

If the boy does not unanimously pass the Board of Review, they will explain the reasons for the failure and discuss how he may meet the requirements — and a follow-up letter will be sent to the scout with these details. (The Board of Review may be put on hold and reconvened at a later date; or an appeal must be done at the next level.)

After unanimously passing the Board of Review, the materials including an advancement report are returned to the council service center, where the application is signed by the executive verifying that the procedures and requirements were followed. Then the application is entered into the national computer system called ScoutNET at the council service center to double-check the signatures and dates and to verify that the procedures and requirements were followed. If okay, the Eagle Scout certificate is sent to the local council center. This process may take several weeks. The date of the Eagle Scout Board of Review is used for any Eagle Scout credentials.

The Eagle Court of Honor

The recognition of the new Eagle Scout is not done in the common Court of Honor, but an individual formal event is planned to highlight the great achievement. The troop committee and the family may schedule and organize the special Eagle Court of Honor. Generally it is for a single boy, but in some cases, such as for brothers or cousins, a joint ceremony may be held. The event should be dignified and enjoyable so it will inspire the other boys to complete their Eagle rank.

The Eagle Court of Honor (or any presentation of the Eagle rank) should not be done until the local council receives the Eagle Scout credentials. You may need to order the official Eagle Presentation Kit from the council service center as soon as the application has its final approval.

It is often a good idea to have someone other than the scout's mother do refreshments and decorations (so she can enjoy in the recognition too). Planning may be assisted by the PLC and the Troop Ladies Auxiliary. The scouts, parents, and leaders should be involved in planning.

The badges and pins should be removed from the presentation box before the ceremony. You may want to bring a guest sign-in book. Other items and tasks to consider in preparation include: PA (public address system), order mother's pin and father's tie tack, decorations, refreshments, photos, notebook, slideshow, displays and props (for presentation during the event or for viewing before and after), write notes/bio for the presenter, agenda, guest invitations, printed program, and selecting a master of ceremonies and a presenter. The presenter is commonly someone of significance to the boy, such as his Scoutmaster, who may discuss (at the event) the importance of the Eagle rank and about the boy's qualifications or character traits.

The event may optionally include a personalized cake, napkins, and program covers with Eagle emblems or red, white, and blue decorations. You may want to ask the council and local scouting store if they have decorations.

The boy should invite special attendees, and counselors and other leaders who helped him through the years. Letters may be sent to dignitaries (such as U.S. president, local congressmen, governor, and mayor) a few weeks in advance to tell them about the accomplishment and to invite them to the ceremony. In many cases, their offices may send letters of recognition and congratulations which may be displayed or read at the event. Also publicity may be done by sending a letter or press release to a local newspaper and for the chartering organization's newsletter.

The event itself generally follows these steps:

- Orderly opening.

- Introduction of candidate by respected leader. (Maybe a quick bio about the boy.)

- Explanation of the Eagle requirements and project.

- Maybe a quick slide show about the boy's scouting participation and/or the Eagle project.

- Parents escorted to front of room to be with the candidate.

- Invite previous Eagle Scouts (including adults) to sit in the Eagle Court (assigned seating section for honoring Eagle Scouts).

- Boy recites the Scout Oath or participates with the Eagle Charge.

- Eagle badge pinned onto the boy's uniform by parent, presenter, Scoutmaster, or troop committee member.

- Parents receive recognition from the boy (a pin and tie tack for example).

- Reading excerpts of congratulatory letters.

- Eagle scout talks if desired.

- Orderly closing.

- Refreshments (such as cake and punch).

Some troops award an official Eagle Scout neckerchief and also an optional National Eagle Scout Association (NESA) membership may be presented. (NESA is an alumni association with membership fees. They provide the *Eagle Scout Magazine* that keeps the members informed about scouting. NESA also offers scholarships. The NESA website is at `http://www.nesa.org/`.) The Eagle Court of Honor should not last too long.

The costs depend on how much is done. Sometimes, the troop pays for the Eagle Presentation Kit. The family may receive sales pitches for Eagle memorabilia and gifts; this is optional and not needed for the ceremony or recognition.

After the Eagle

The Eagle is not the end of the road — scouts should and do continue active participation in scouting. As youth, the boys can continue to earn merit badges (and Eagle Palms), go camping and on high adventures, and attend meetings. They may work on various awards as introduced in chapter 9. The boys should continue to be leaders (such as a Troop Guide, Instructor, or Junior Assistant Scoutmaster) by sharing their experience with younger scouts and helping plan and lead meetings and activities. The scout may participate in Order of the Arrow (if a member) or join Varsity Scouts or Venturing. He may work at resident camps, take more training courses, and attend Philmont, camporees, and Jamborees, etc.

Scouting is lifelong and the opportunities are endless. When becoming an adult, with proper registration, he may be able to continue service as an adult leader or committee member. (See pages 29 and 33 for more ideas.)

Eagle Palms

Before a boy turns 18 years old, he may earn Eagle Palms. A pin is awarded for participation for three months and completing more merit badges (the scout has at least 26). The Bronze palm is for five, Gold for ten, and then Silver for 15 additional merit badges. The scout will participate in a Scoutmaster conference and complete a Board of Review for each palm. The boy may be formally recognized at a normal troop Court of Honor. The pins are worn on the Eagle knot or Eagle badge ribbon in the minimum combination to show count of merit badges beyond Eagle.

Summary

- Earning the Eagle requires many documented procedural steps that should be followed precisely, such as using official paperwork and getting approvals signed in the correct order and by the correct people.

- The Eagle Scout Leadership Service Project, which benefits the community or non-profit organization, is planned, developed, organized, led, and documented by the boy.

- The completed Eagle Scout Rank Application and the Eagle Scout Leadership Service Project Workbook are submitted in preparation for a special Eagle Board of Review, which may be held by the local council or district.

Index

CPSIA information can be obtained
at www.ICGtesting.com
Printed in the USA
BVHW031535130320
574963BV00004B/594